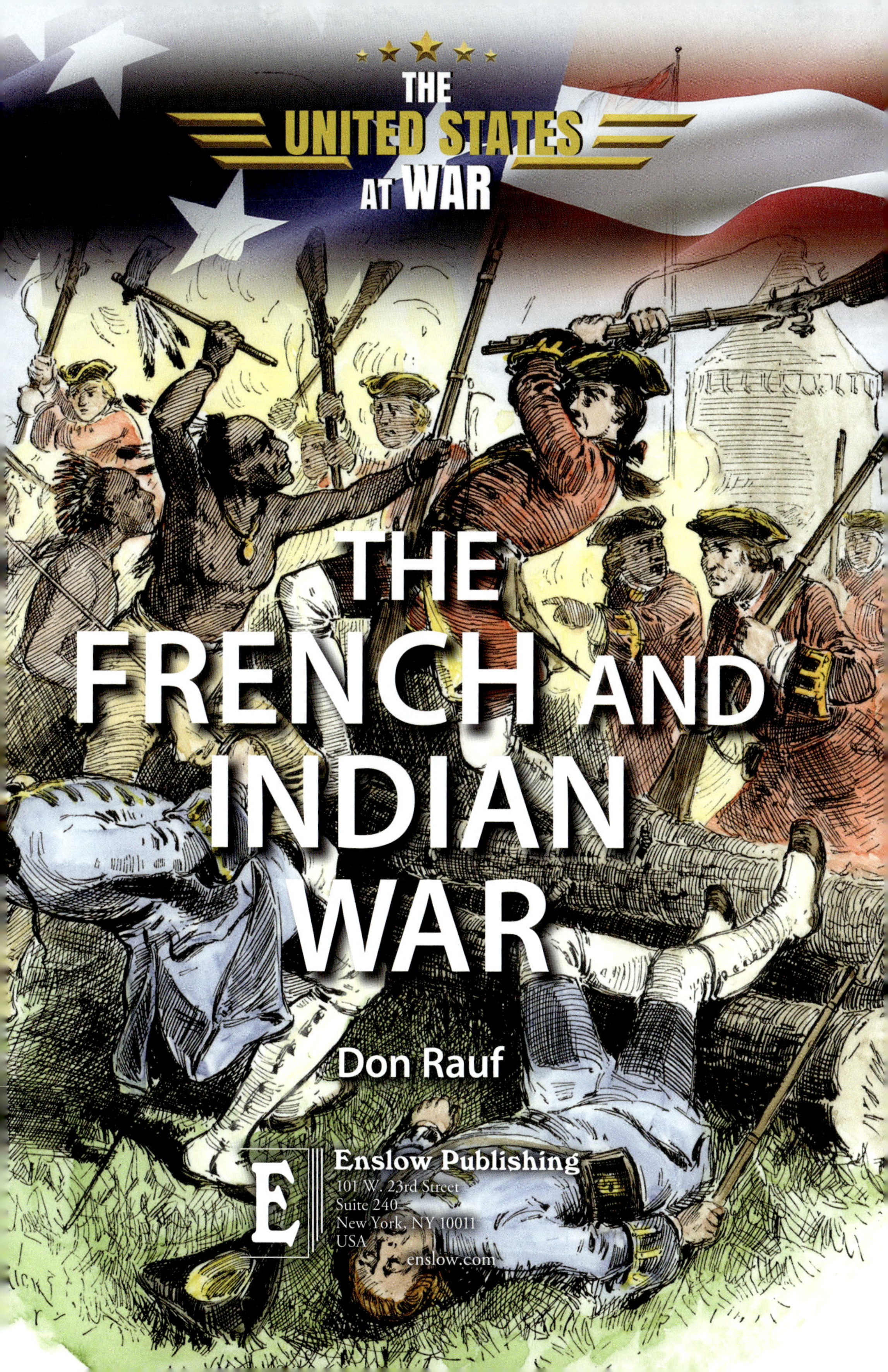

THE UNITED STATES AT WAR

THE FRENCH AND INDIAN WAR

Don Rauf

Enslow Publishing
101 W. 23rd Street
Suite 240
New York, NY 10011
USA
enslow.com

Published in 2017 by Enslow Publishing, LLC.
101 W. 23rd Street, Suite 240, New York, NY 10011

Library of Congress Cataloging-in-Publication Data
Names: Rauf, Don, author.
Title: The French and Indian War / Don Rauf.
Description: New York, NY : Enslow Publishing, 2017 | Series: The United States at war | Includes bibliographical references and index.
Identifiers: LCCN 2016004686 | ISBN 9780766076761 (library bound)
Subjects: LCSH: United States—History—French and Indian War, 1754-1763. | Canada—History—1755-1763.
Classification: LCC E199 .R24 2017 | DDC 973.2/6—dc23
LC record available at http://lccn.loc.gov/2016004686

Printed in the United States of America

To Our Readers: We have done our best to make sure all websites in this book were active and appropriate when we went to press. However, the author and the publisher have no control over and assume no liability for the material available on those websites or on any websites they may link to. Any comments or suggestions can be sent by e-mail to customerservice@enslow.com.

Photo Credits: Cover, p. 1, Memory Stockphoto/Shutterstock.com (insignia), Sergey Kamshylin/Shutterstock.com (US flag); © North Wind Picture Archives/Alamy Stock Photo; pp. 4–5 DEA PICTURE LIBRARY/De Agostini Picture Library/Getty Images; pp. 6, 74, 96 Print Collector/Hulton Archive/Getty Images; p. 8 PHAS/Universal Images Group/Getty Images; p.11 Private Collection/Ken Welsh/Bridgeman Images; p. 15 Private Collection/Peter Newark American Pictures/Bridgeman Images; p. 18 Private Collection/Photo © Christie's Images/Bridgeman Images; p. 22 Interim Archives/Archive Photos/Getty Images; p. 28 meunierd/Shutterstock.com; p. 31 VHS accession number: 1849.1/Virginia Historical Society; p. 34 Bob Thomas/Popperfoto/Getty Images; p. 38 Ashmolean Museum, University of Oxford, UK/Bridgeman Images; p. 42 Everett Historical/Shutterstock.com; p. 46 © North Wind Picture Archives/Alamy Stock Photo; pp. 48, 85 Universal History Archive/Universal Images Group/Getty Images; pp. 56, 72 © North Wind Picture Archives; p. 59 SuperStock/Getty Images; pp. 62, 109 Kean Collection/Archive Photos/Getty Images; p. 64 Bibliotheque Nationale, Paris,France/Bridgeman Images; p. 68 Stock Montage/Archive Photos/Getty Images; p. 78 © Classic Image/Alamy Stock Photo; p. 80 © Ivy Close Images/Alamy Stock Photo; p. 86 © Gerry Embleton/North Wind Picture Archives; p. 88 Private Collection/©Look and Learn/Bridgeman Images; p. 90 Benson Lossing/Fort Niagara II.jpg/Wikimedia commons; p. 98 Ashmolean Museum,University of Oxford, UK/Bridgeman Images; p. 102 Private Collection/Peter Newark American Pictures/Bridgeman Images; p.112 French School/Archives du Ministere des Affaires Etrangeres,Paris,France/Archives Charmet/Bridgeman Images; p.115 National Army Museum, London/Bridgeman Images.

CONTENTS

FOREWORD 4

CHAPTER 1
Coming to America 6

CHAPTER 2
The Settlements Grow 22

CHAPTER 3
George Washington Ignites a War 34

CHAPTER 4
A Storm on the Horizon 46

CHAPTER 5
The Shifting Balance of Power 62

CHAPTER 6
The British Star Rises 74

CHAPTER 7
The Fall of New France 88

CHAPTER 8
The Final Stages 102

Chronology 116

Chapter Notes 119

Glossary 124

For More Information 125

Index 126

FOREWORD

When I was in grade school, lessons about early American history mostly focused on the Revolution. Although there was mention of the French and Indian War, which came before, it was always brief, almost a footnote. Because I grew up in upstate New York, we'd take trips to Lake George and Lake Champlain. Historical plaques and forts from the 1700s made me more aware of the great battles between the French and British that had been fought there. It was hard to image that these peaceful bodies of water, where people now came to vacation, were fiercely contested areas. It was hard to picture Lake George filled with a massive flotilla of boats carrying hundreds of British redcoats and colonials. On a longer vacation to nearby Montreal, Quebec, in Canada, I wondered why there were so many French-speakers in this part of the country. It all went back to the French and Indian War.

France and England were the predominant settlers of North America at the time and as they expanded their territories, friction was bound to happen. As France and England used North America as a battleground, another peoples got caught in the crossfire—the Native American Indians. While the Indians were often allied with the French, especially early in the war, some tribes came to terms with the British as well. For the most part, Native Americans just wanted to maintain the lands where they had lived for centuries. They allied with the people they thought were most likely to help them keep these lands and maintain their way of life. Having the opportunity to write this book made it clear how influential the French and Indian War was. The long war would sow the seeds for the American Revolution, and shape the culture of the continent that we have to this day.

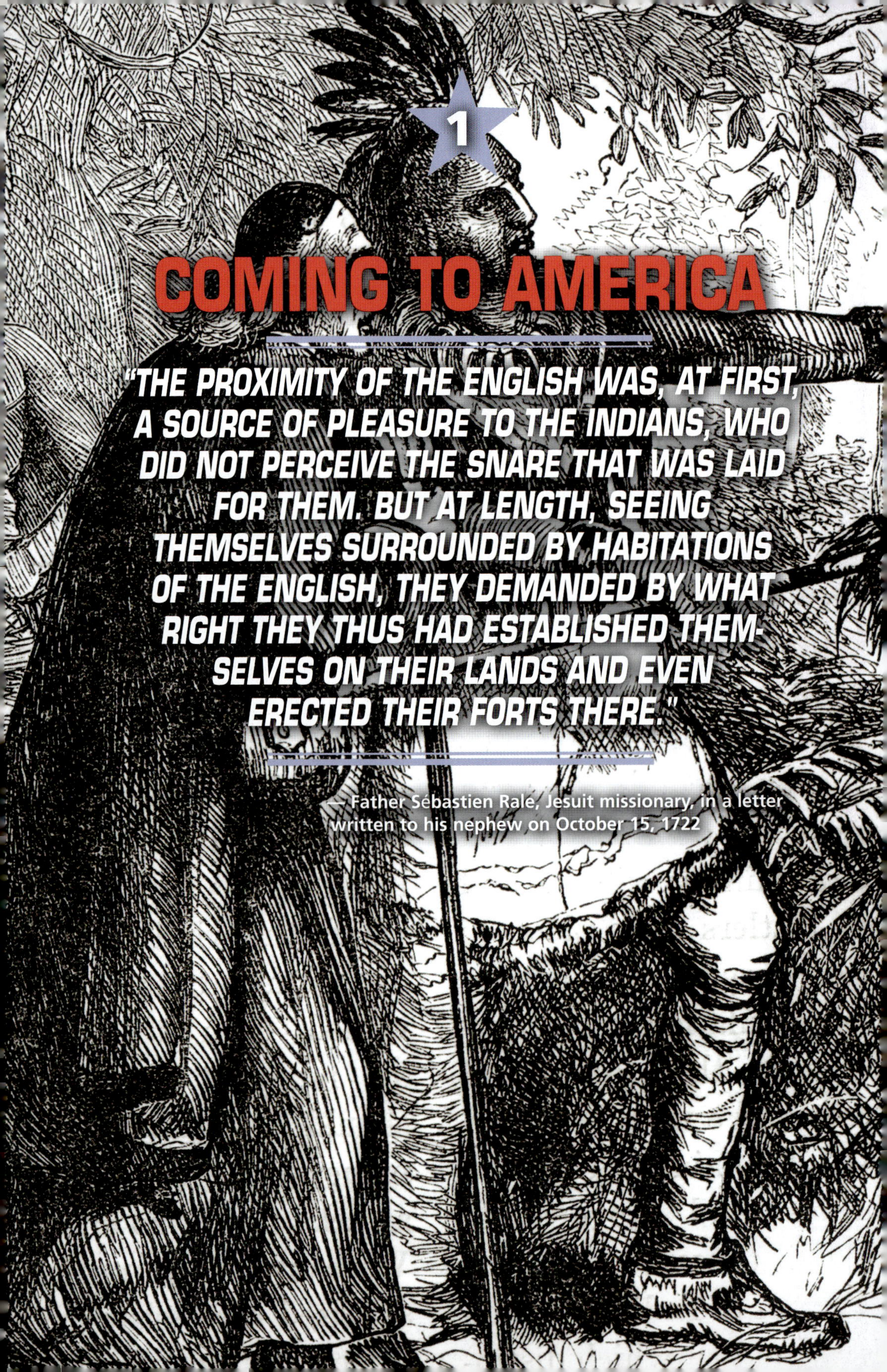

1

COMING TO AMERICA

"THE PROXIMITY OF THE ENGLISH WAS, AT FIRST, A SOURCE OF PLEASURE TO THE INDIANS, WHO DID NOT PERCEIVE THE SNARE THAT WAS LAID FOR THEM. BUT AT LENGTH, SEEING THEMSELVES SURROUNDED BY HABITATIONS OF THE ENGLISH, THEY DEMANDED BY WHAT RIGHT THEY THUS HAD ESTABLISHED THEM-SELVES ON THEIR LANDS AND EVEN ERECTED THEIR FORTS THERE."

— Father Sébastien Rale, Jesuit missionary, in a letter written to his nephew on October 15, 1722

While the French and Indian War officially started in 1754 and ended in 1763, this lengthy conflict between France and England had begun to simmer decades before that. The conflict was not just about North America, either. In the bigger picture, it was just one piece of a larger, very long-term conflict between these two superpowers. Britain and France had already been on opposite sides in several wars before the very bloody North American war broke out.

The history of the war can be traced back to the Age of Discovery when the countries of Europe were putting a large amount of resources into looking for alternate trade routes to Asia and the Far East. By the middle of 1400s, the Ottoman Empire, also called the Turkish Empire, controlled many of the trade connections between Europe and Asia. Spices, herbs, incense, silk and other products of the East were highly desirable in the West. So European kingdoms began to look for new ways to get to Asia to avoid having to go through the Ottoman Empire. Spain funded Christopher Columbus's famous expedition in 1492 for this reason. Instead of finding a route to Asia, though, Columbus found North America, a continent Europeans did not know existed at that time.

Martin Frobisher was a seaman who explored for England in the 1500s.

Five years later, King Henry VII of England sent John Cabot to North America to look for the Northwest Passage, a route across the Atlantic that they hoped would eventually connect to the Pacific Ocean in order to establish trade with East Asia. On his voyages, Cabot would claim land around Nova Scotia and Maine for the English Crown. England didn't follow up on Cabot's initial explorations until the 1570s when Queen Elizabeth I sent Sir Martin Frobisher on three voyages to the New World, also to find the Northwest Passage. He landed in the northeastern part of Canada and thought he had struck it rich when he shipped back 200 tons of what he thought was gold, but it turned out to be iron pyrite, also called fool's gold.[1]

Around this same time, from 1534 to 1535, Jacques Cartier established a foothold for France along the St. Lawrence River, extending east from the Atlantic Ocean inland to Montreal in Canada. He mapped and explored the areas from present-day Newfoundland and Montreal, and made connections with the native people living in the region.

The Spanish, of course, were in the exploration game as well. In the years between 1539 to 1542, Francisco Vazquez de Coronado brought Spanish settlers to the American Southwest and Hernando de Soto opened areas in Florida, Georgia, and Alabama to the Spanish.[2]

In 1607, the British established their first colony in Jamestown, Virginia. By 1608, the French had established the colony of Quebec, which became its economic and political center in North America, and a key location for establishing relationships with many Indian groups in the St. Lawrence River valley and the Great Lakes area.

In 1609, the Dutch entered the scene also looking to expand their empire. Although he was an Englishman, Henry Hudson sailed for both the Netherlands and the Dutch East India Company. Under their flags, he guided his ship the *Half Moon* up the Hudson River. The Dutch started the colony of New Amsterdam at the mouth of the Hudson River in 1625. About forty years later, however, the English took New Amsterdam from the Dutch. The Dutch settlers, under the leadership of Peter Stuyvesant, swore allegiance to England rather than trying to fight. So New Amsterdam transformed into New York—which we now know as New York City.[3]

Early Friction Between French and British

Troubles between the British and French in North America were already stirring in 1654. At this time the French were living in the region of Eastern Maine, New Brunswick, and Nova Scotia called Acadia. British settlers, urged on by Lord Protector Oliver Cromwell, captured the region. But the British returned Acadia to France in 1667, under the monarchy of the pro-Catholic Charles II. As Catholicism was the predominant religion in France, the two nations maintained a peaceful coexistence until Protestant William III took the throne in 1688. Within no time, the two nations were at war.[4]

The Dutch surrendered New Amsterdam to the British on September 8, 1664.

On April 9, 1682, René-Robert Cavelier, Sieur de La Salle and his men reached the Gulf of Mexico after traveling down the Mississippi by canoe. They declared the entire Mississippi Basin for France and named it Louisiana in honor of the king, Louis XIV. France controlled the major waterways of the Mississippi, the St. Lawrence River, and the Great Lakes, along which they built a string of trading posts. New France concentrated development in Canada along the St. Lawrence River, in the Illinois Country (mid-Mississippi Valley) and Louisiana (New Orleans and some areas west of the Mississippi). Spain maintained control of Florida, Texas, New Mexico, and California. By the early half of the 18th century, England had established thirteen colonies along the East Coast of America.

Living Among the Indigenous People

It is important to keep in mind that as the European nations came declaring lands for themselves, there were people already living there—the Native Americans. At the time that Columbus arrived in North America, the native population was estimated at ten million.[5] (About half that number live in the United States today, and indigenous people of Canada number about 900,000.) The original people of North America were named "Indians" because Christopher

Columbus and other early explorers thought they had reached the Indian Ocean.

At this time, the Europeans were relatively few in number. In 1700, there were about 250,000 Europeans in America, 15,000 in New France, and 4,500 settlers from Spain.[6]

Initially, the white settlers and the Indians may have feared each other. In time, however, trade was established. Europeans would take beaver pelts, buffalo robes, and other items in exchange for ammunition, metals, textiles, and glass products. Making gifts to the Indians was also an effective way of keeping the peace and opening relations.

The French, especially, thought cooperation and understanding were the best ways to live harmoniously with the Indians, while developing a lucrative fur trade and fishing industry. The French Jesuits were especially effective at winning the trust of the native people. The Jesuits were Catholic missionaries who wanted to convert Indians to the Catholic religion.

The French were interested in Indian life and culture. They befriended many of the numerous tribes, including the Chippewas, the Algonquins, the Cherokees, the Creeks, and Sioux. The Jesuits made connections with many Iroquois, Mohawks, Cayugas, Senecas, and Onondagas. There were more than two hundred tribes speaking more than two hundred different languages. The French learned to speak many of these native languages. In time, the French married Indian women as well, strengthening the connection between their people.

They also accompanied tribesmen into battles, often dressing like them. The French learned to fight in a more savage manner, frequently launching surprise attacks from the cover of the woods rather than engaging in regimented battle. Some French learned to kill from behind and practiced scalping just as the Indians did.

The "Black Robes," as the Jesuits were called, did not demand that Indians abandon their heritage. In the St. Lawrence valley, missionaries set up "praying villages," where Indians could observe Catholicism, but still uphold their cultural ways. Father Sébastien Rale spent thirty years among the Abenaki Indians of Norridgewock, Maine, from about 1694 to 1726. He learned their customs and language and wrote an Abenaki-French dictionary. The Abenaki would often side with the French during the French and Indian War.[7]

As the French built their trust, the Native Americans increasingly participated in the lucrative fur trade. France established forts in the Upper Great Lakes and St. Lawrence areas that made it easy to trade for goods and helped solidify relations. The French seemed to be a beneficial partner to the Native Americans rather than a threat. The French, who were largely working the fur trade, also were more transitory.

A French missionary preaches to some Algonquin Indians. Some Native Americans adopted Christianity after hearing Jesuit teachings.

Unlike the English, they were not putting down expansive permanent roots on Indian hunting grounds.

The British settlers (as well as many German, Dutch, and Swedes) took a less friendly stance toward the Native Americans. They often regarded the Indian as savages or animals, rather than people with their own traditions and a deeper culture. However, over time, the English did make some Native American allies.

Though the French had good relationships with many native groups, they were not friendly with all of them—in particular, the Iroquois. When French explorer Samuel Champlain founded Quebec in 1608, he decided to make allies with the Huron Indians to build a fur trade. The Hurons, however, were enemies with the Iroquois. Champlain and his men even fought alongside the Hurons against the Iroquois.

The Iroquois did not forget.[8] In the 1700s, the Iroquois had formed a powerful federation with related Native American nations. The Senecas, Oneidas, Onondagas, Mohawks, Cayugas, and Tuscaroras formed the Iroquois Confederacy, or Six Nations (also called the Haudenosaunee). The Six Nations became a powerful English ally, although allegiances would shift depending on the situation. The Mohawks in the East of New York were more likely to deal with the English, while the Seneca along Lakes Ontario and Erie would often conduct business with the French.

Battles in Europe Spill Over to America

In late 1600s and early 1700s, the nations of Europe were at war. From 1688 to 1697, England was fighting the War of the League of Augsburg. In this conflict, Louis XIV of France was pushing to expand his country's territory to take over the Hapsburgs of Austria. Also known as the Nine Years' War or the War of the Grand Alliance, England joined Sweden, Spain, Austria, Holland, and a few German states to keep France from expanding. Ultimately, the Hapsburgs lost areas to Louis XIV.

In America, the French and British fought as part of the war effort as well. Here, the fighting was called King William's War, named after England's monarch King William III. Toward the end of the seventeenth century, the French governor of Canada, Louis de Buade de Frontenac, instigated several attacks on the British, pushing them down from the North. In 1689, he persuaded Iroquois Indians to attack Major Richard Waldron and the other citizens of Dover, New Hampshire. The Iroquois were motivated to strike because thirteen years before, Waldron had taken some 400 Indians prisoner. He had tricked them by inviting them to

King William III is pictured during a battle in the Nine Years' War.

participate in a mock battle with local militiamen. When the Indians were gathered together, Waldron and his men held them captive. Many of the Indians were sold into slavery or executed. At the end of June 1689, the Indians took over the town and killed many settlers.[9]

In another attack in 1690, now known as The Schenectady Massacre, French and Indian raiders burned the town of Schenectady in upstate New York. More than sixty Dutch and English inhabitants were killed. Other towns in New England and New York met similar fates. In retaliation, the colonies assembled two thousand men whose goal was to penetrate Montreal via Lake Champlain, and thirty to forty ships aimed at destroying Quebec. But Governor Frontenac's forces repelled both the land forces, and those coming by ship. Although Sir William Phips of Maine captured Port Royal in Nova Scotia in this battle, the military attack on "New France" was ineffective and monetarily costly for the colonists. Skirmishes continued with bloody battles in York, Maine; Durham, New Hampshire; and Groton, Massachusetts. Both the French and English lacked resources for a full-scale war. A truce was struck in 1697 with the Treaty of Ryswick in Europe, and was followed, in 1699, by a truce in North America.

A War Against a French-Spanish Alliance

An uneasy peace would last for about three years. Once again, troubles in Europe were brewing that would lead to conflict in America. King Charles II of Spain ruled over an extensive realm, including land in the Americas. Charles had no son, so European powers were concerned about who would become the next King of Spain. On his deathbed, Charles chose the sixteen-year-old Philip, Duke of Anjou. Philip was a grandson of Louis XIV of France and a great grandson of Philip IV, a former king of Spain. When Charles died on November 1, 1700, Philip V became king of Spain. Although Philip renounced all claims to becoming the monarch of France as well, France and Spain now had strong ties to each other, making them threatening to other European nations. To fight this threat, William III of England put together the Great Alliance of England in 1701, including Holland, Prussia,

Austria, Portugal, and most of the Holy Roman Empire states (regions controlled mainly by German princes). They believed that a member of the Austrian Hapsburg family should be the rightful heir to the Spanish throne. When William III died in 1702, Queen Anne took over the throne and began the War of the Spanish Succession.[10]

In America, this conflict was called Queen Anne's War, and combat soon began there as well. With the struggle going on in Europe, England saw Spanish and French settlements in America as a threat. In 1704, British colonists overpowered French settlements at Minas and Beaubassin in Nova Scotia. Eventually the British would take over all of Nova Scotia. Because it had some of the richest fishing grounds known to man, Nova Scotia was a treasured prize.

The French also had their share of victory. That same year (1704) under cold heavy snows at the end of February, the French, with the help of Native American allies, destroyed Deerfield, Massachusetts, killing fifty men, women, and children. More than 100 captured residents were forced to march to Canada, and about twenty died from exhaustion and extreme conditions. The town of Deerfield was burned to the ground. The French also razed Haverhill, Massachusetts, and took the English colony of Bonavista in Newfoundland.

In the south, the British had successes in St. Augustine, Florida in 1702, and destroyed several Spanish missions throughout northwestern Florida in 1704.

By 1713, nations were tiring of war and Louis XIV was able to use diplomacy to establish terms to end the fighting. The war officially ended with the signing the Treaty of Utrecht. Philip would remain king of Spain under the promise that Spain and France would never unite.

In the treaty, England gained most of Nova Scotia and Newfoundland, the southern shores of the Hudson Bay, and the Island of St. Kitts in the Caribbean. The French kept Cape Breton Island, in northern Nova Scotia. Here the French had built Fort Louisbourg, which was New France's most important port after Quebec. Fort Louisbourg gave France a vital position to travel the St. Lawrence River and gave it access to all the settlements inland. Cod fishing and the fur trade flourished, and both industries brought more wealth into France. Although most of Nova Scotia was now nominally under British control, most of the inhabitants were French colonists called Acadians.

2

THE SETTLEMENTS GROW

"IT IS OF THE UTMOST IMPORTANCE AND OF ABSOLUTE NECESSITY TO SECURE CANADA."

— Marquis de la Galissonnière, Governor of New France, December 1750

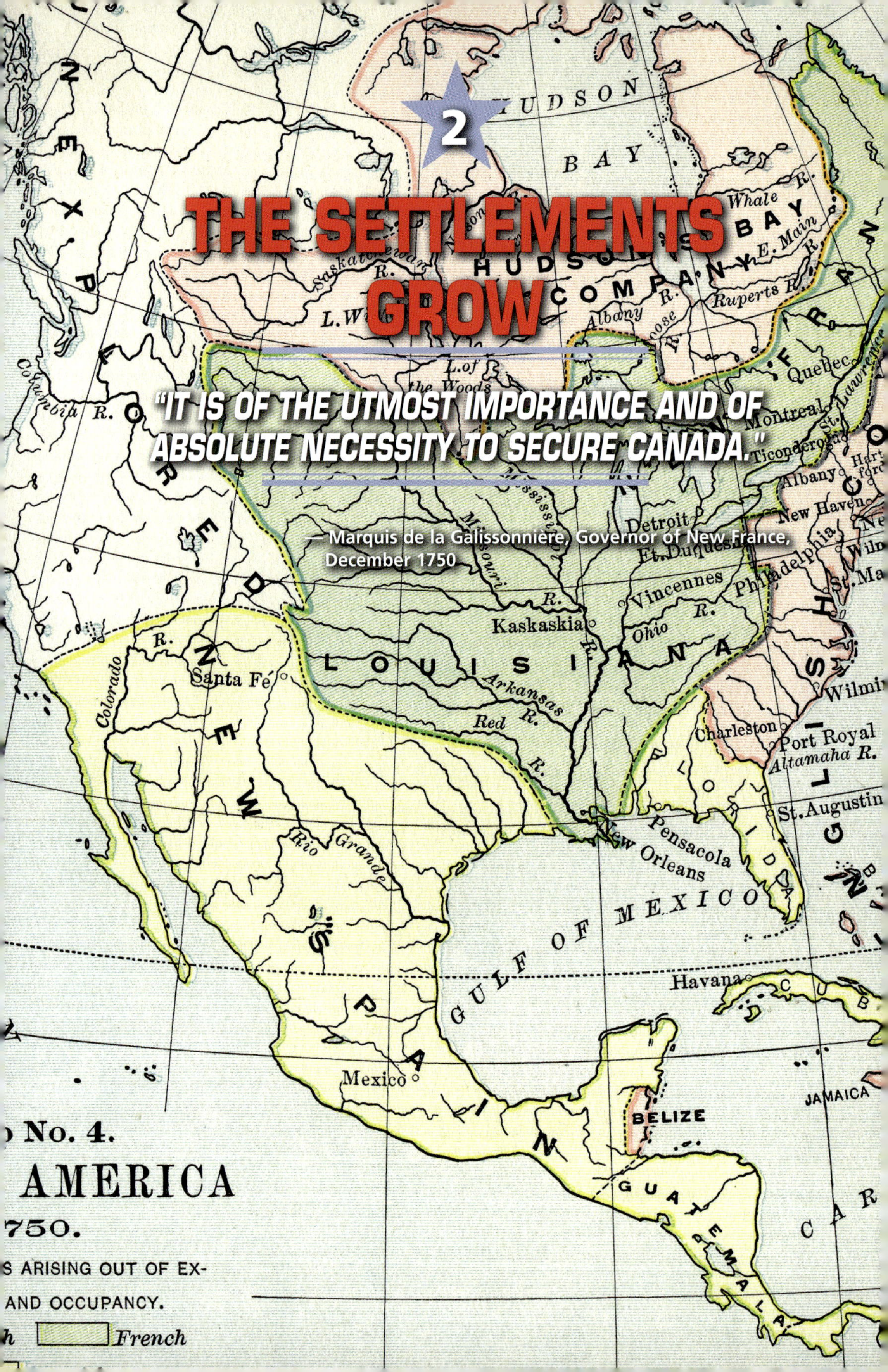

The French established New Orleans in 1718. The city sits at the Mississippi River's mouth. Many French Catholics settled here. These French Catholics did not share the more severe view of life held by the New England Puritan colonists. While religious, the French Catholics were known to enjoy good food and lively music. New Orleans remains a culturally unique city today because of the major French Catholic influence there.

Meanwhile, the English colonies also continued to expand rapidly, reaching a population of 475,000 in 1720. The steady influx of people would be one of England's advantages when the French and Indian War started. By the mid-1700s, the numbers were more than double what they were in 1720 with 1.1 million white settlers plus 300,000 slaves living in the English colonies. In New France, French settlers only numbered 60,000. The Spanish colonies had about 19,000.[1]

To a large degree, the population swells in the British colonies were greater because they were more inclusive—they accepted Germans, Swedes, Dutch and other nationalities along with English, Scotch, and Irish. The French and Spanish, however, limited immigration to Roman Catholics. For example, French Protestants known as Huguenots were exiled from Catholic France and not welcome in New France. Several hundred thousand Huguenots made their home in the English colonies, where they were free to practice whatever religion they wished. This policy of exclusion would play a major role in France's eventual failure in North America. Without their Indian allies, the French would not have lasted as long as they did.

England also concentrated on strengthening its Navy. In the years to come, the British would dominate the oceans and become the world's greatest sea power.

To bolster its position in North America, France built and reinforced its forts. To control access to the Great Lakes and establish a base for the fur trade, the French had previously constructed Fort Niagara near Niagara Falls. The French further fortified this location, as well as their holdings along the lower Ohio River and Wabash River. (The Wabash flows into the Ohio River and the Ohio River feeds into the Mississippi.) In 1734, the French set up Fort Saint-Frédéric on Lake Champlain to help secure New France from British encroachment. Located in Crown Point, New York, the British felt this fort was an intrusion into their territory. The French were inching further southward, coming too close for comfort.

The War of Jenkin's Ear

France wasn't the only one causing the British concern. In the south, the growing Spanish influence in Florida and French in Louisiana prompted England to give General James Oglethorpe the authority to establish the settlement of Savannah, Georgia, in 1733. The state would serve as a buffer between the Spanish colonists to the south and the established English colonies to the north. Tensions between Spain and England rose until a war erupted over the tip of a smuggler's ear. A Spanish privateer had a confrontation with a British sea captain (possibly a British pirate) named Robert Jenkins and severed his ear with a blade. The incident happened in 1731 and at first it had little impact, but the episode became a vivid symbol of Spanish barbarity toward the English. Hostilities between Georgia and Florida grew, leading to fighting in 1739. The ongoing fighting was called the War of Jenkin's Ear.[2] Oglethorpe launched an unsuccessful siege on St. Augustine a year later. The Spaniards retaliated with an invasion in Frederica, called the Battle of Bloody Marsh in 1742. The War of Jenkin's Ear got caught up in the larger European war that broke out around the same time, called King George's War in America.

Yet Another European War Erupts in America

Before the French and Indian War could yet begin, another conflict in Europe sent New France and British America back into battle. King Charles VI, emperor of Austria, died in 1740. His eldest daughter, Maria Theresa took the throne but Frederick II of Prussia (which included parts of present-day Poland and most of Germany) did not respect Maria's ascension in Austria and launched the War of the Austrian Succession.[3] Prussia allied with France, which saw this conflict as an opportunity to gain territory for itself. When Prussia took over an area of Austria called Silesia in December 1740, the war was on. Taken off guard at first, Maria Theresa of Austria was not prepared to fight, but soon she made an alliance with England.

With England and France now on opposite sides in this war, the two perpetual enemies resumed their struggle in America, continuing King George's War. Again, both the French and the English carried out bloody raids. For France, it was an opportunity to try to reclaim a major loss to the British: Nova Scotia.

A Fight Among the Fisheries

In 1745, the French took over several fisheries that were in the "New England" portion of Nova Scotia. They then set their sights on Britain's Nova Scotia outpost, Annapolis Royal. The local Mi`kmaq Indians aided the French, leading the first strike on this British settlement. Governor William Shirley of Massachusetts anticipated that France would keep attacking to the south if they were not blocked. With the arrival of Shirley and about 200 of his men, the Mi`kmaq were driven off in July 1745. In August, a force of French and Indians together descended on Annapolis Royal, but ultimately the siege was thwarted.

Britain then decided to take the initiative. The French stronghold of Louisbourg was a continuing threat to the New Englanders, but it was heavily protected with 1,500 men and cannons. The New England clergy called it the "Stronghold of Satan." France never thought

This mural shows the Mi'kmaq Indians of Nova Scotia.

that untrained colonists could overcome the soldiers Fort Louisbourg, so they were totally surprised when a force of about 4,000 men, with help from a Royal Navy Squadron, defeated them in the summer of 1745. Their leader, William Pepperrell, a merchant from Kittery, Maine, was celebrated as a hero. London and the colonies celebrated the hard-won triumph. Because New England had made such a sacrifice in the battle, the people there were understandably disappointed when Fort Louisbourg was eventually returned to the French.[4] The Treaty of Aix-la-Chapelle in 1748 ended King George's War, and returned all colonial claims to their previous owners. Britain and Spain unofficially agreed upon St. Johns River as the boundary between Georgia and Florida, also ending the War of Jenkin's Ear.

Just Getting Warmed Up

With all the skirmishes, battles, and raids that had occurred between the French and British up until this point, it would seem that the French and Indian War had already been going on for decades in North America. All this fighting, however, was just the warm-up for the big conflict—a war that would decide once and for all who would control North America.

Even after the end of King George's War, the third conflict between the French and British, tension between the two countries continued in America. France continued to control the vital waterways of the Mississippi and St. Lawrence Rivers, but the population in the English colonies was growing rapidly and expanding westward. Settlers came over the Appalachian Mountains into uncharted territory, pushing more and more against the French. The kettle of war was simmering but it had yet to reach full boil.

In 1744, the Iroquois signed the Treaty of Lancaster, which gave their land in Maryland and Virginia to the British. This allowed the Virginia House of Burgesses (the first democratically elected legislative body in the British American colonies) to grant western land to Virginia-based land companies in 1745. The British were able to thrust further westward.

On March 27, 1749, King George II of England granted huge tracts of land in the Ohio Valley to a group of entrepreneurs called the Ohio Company.[5] Lieutenant Governor Robert Dinwiddie of Virginia had significant financial interest in this business. The Ohio Company was instructed to build a settlement of 100 families with a fort to protect them within seven years. The Ohio Company was also making alliances with local Indians and gaining some support.

Marking Their Territory

As the English began to stream into the Ohio Valley, the governor of New France Roland-Michel Barrin de La Galissonnière grew more concerned. He encouraged France to send more people to populate New France. He also reached out to gain as much good will as possible from the Native Americans.

Galissonnière wanted to make it clear beyond a shadow of a doubt that all regions around the Ohio River and its tributaries belonged to France—English settlers there would have to move out. The French had a common practice of burying plates to show land ownership, which first began in Europe in the Middle Ages. He decided that plaques such as these must be put on the land in the Ohio Valley to clearly show France's claim to the area.

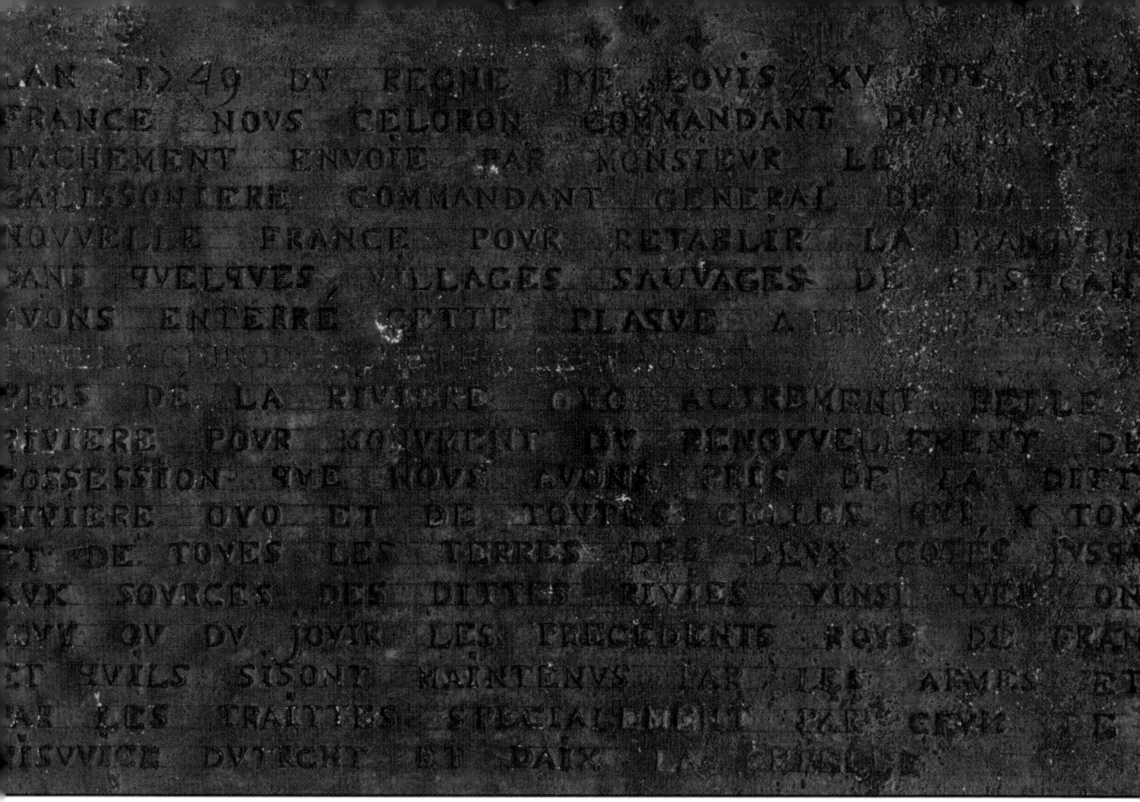

This plate was planted at the place where the Kanawha and Ohio rivers joined by Céloron. It is the only plate that survived.

In the spring of 1749, Galissonnière sent Captain Pierre-Joseph Céloron de Blainville and 213 men (including Indians) down the Allegheny and Ohio Rivers to carry out this mission. Along their 3,000-mile (4,828-kilometers) journey, Céloron and his crew buried lead plates inscribed with France's claim to the territory.[6] The plaques stated that the French land claims were upheld by the European treaties of Ryswick, Utrecht, and Aix-la-Chapelle.

In total, Céloron is believed to have buried at least six plates. Only one has been found intact. As Céloron traveled from Pittsburgh to the Great Miami River, he came in contact with a large number of British traders. Although he warned them that they must leave, the traders largely ignored him. His efforts to reestablish relations with Indians in these areas were also not very fruitful. The English had been selling the Indians goods at a fraction of the cost charged by the French. French traders quickly moved into the region to reestablish a presence there, with the hopes of strengthening their relationship with the Native Americans.

In August 1749, however, Galissonnière stepped down as the Governor of New France and handed these problems over to his replacement, the Marquis de La Jonquière. Jonquière quickly realized the challenges ahead—especially with getting support from the home country. In the History of Canada, James Frith Jeffers reports that Jonquière received a salary of just $1,300 a year and he was required to feed and clothe twenty-seven guard soldiers from that allowance. (He did, however, amass a small fortune by selling brandy to the Indians.) By 1751, Jonquière had persuaded France to send more war materials and troops into Quebec. The French also made repairs and strengthened their forts at Frontenac, Toronto, and Detroit.

In 1750, as the Ohio Company plunged ever westward, it chose Christopher Gist—an accomplished colonial British explorer, surveyor, and frontiersman—to survey along the Ohio River headwaters near Pittsburgh. In 1752, Gist was able to negotiate a deal with the Six Nations that gave the English the right to take vast lands in Ohio. But almost as quickly as settlers moved in, the French-allied Indians drove them out.

Jonquière's reign was not long. He died at age 67 on March 17, 1752, in Montreal after months of illness. When Ange Duquesne de Menneville took over as governor of New France, he built a chain of forts stretching from New Orleans to Montreal.[7] Fort Presque Isle sat on Lake Erie at Erie, Pennsylvania. Fort Le Boeuf stood at the head of French Creek in Waterford, Pennsylvania, and Fort Machault sat on the banks of the Allegheny River in Venango County in present-day Franklin. Back in England, Lord Halifax, head of the board of trade in Parliament, was alarmed by these aggressive moves by France. He called for war.

The Iroquois and other Indians, meanwhile, were hemmed in, feeling pressure from both sides. With each passing year, they lost more of their precious hunting grounds.

3

GEORGE WASHINGTON IGNITES A WAR

"THE LAND BELONGS TO NEITHER ONE NOR THE OTHER (FRENCH NOR BRITISH)...SO I DESIRE YOU TO WITHDRAW."

— Half-King Tanacharison, representative of the Iroquois Confederacy of American Indians, to the French Captain at Fort Le Boeuf, December 1753

As the pressure mounted, Governor Robert Dinwiddie of Virginia received authority from Britain to eject the French from any lands deemed to be under the jurisdiction of Virginia. One of the first sites targeted for eviction was Fort Le Boeuf, in what is now northwest Pennsylvania, just south of Lake Erie. To deliver this notification, Dinwiddie chose the seasoned frontiersman Christopher Gist and a young 21-year-old Virginia militia captain. The young captain had very little experience and a minimal amount of schooling.

Yet this 6 foot 2 inch (1.87 meters) soldier had practical experience as a surveyor and had been a major in the Virginia militia previously. His half-brother, Lawrence, had been a respected admiral when he died in 1752, and this young man became the master of the estate called Mount Vernon. The young man was George Washington. Although he was paid just 100 pounds per year, he was eager for the mission.[1]

Washington left Williamsburg, Virginia in October 1753. Along the way, he picked up Jacob van Braam, who spoke French. In November, Washington and his team arrived at Logstown, a cultural center of Indian activity, located just Northwest of modern-day Pittsburgh. Among the Iroquois longhouses and the cabins built by the French, peddlers were busy selling animal furs and firearms. Young Washington had had little exposure to Indians, so he was intrigued by the community which buzzed with the sound of different native languages.

Collaborating With the Indians

Here, at the end of November, Washington met with the native power brokers—the Mingo Half-King Tanacharison, Scarouady, Shingas, and other Indian chiefs. The Iroquois had a system of regional representation whereby "Half-Kings" served as representatives for specific regions.

They spoke on behalf of the Six Nations and conducted business with the British and French.

In their meeting, Washington learned that the Indians were just as unhappy with the encroaching French as they were with the British. The Half-King Tanacharison recently had an unpleasant meeting with the French at Fort Le Boeuf. He made it clear that the French could not take their land by force, but the commander at that time, Pierre-Paul Marin, harshly told Tanacharison that the French would take what land they wanted. The French generally worked well with the Indians but in this instance, a defiant, hostile tone worked against them.

Washington attempted to broker an alliance with the Indians, but the Indians were not willing to commit to any agreement. Washington, however, had made a favorable impression, and Tanacharison and three of his men agreed to accompany Washington and his team to Fort Le Boeuf. Tanacharison said that he would bring a wampum belt, which was an official token that Indians used to confirm and record a treaty between parties. Wampum belts were made of shells strung together. Tanacharison's wampum was special. This black and white wampum belt served as a final warning for the French to leave.

Rebuffed at Fort Le Boeuf

Taking the matter as a very serious diplomatic venture, Washington arrived at Fort Le Boeuf in

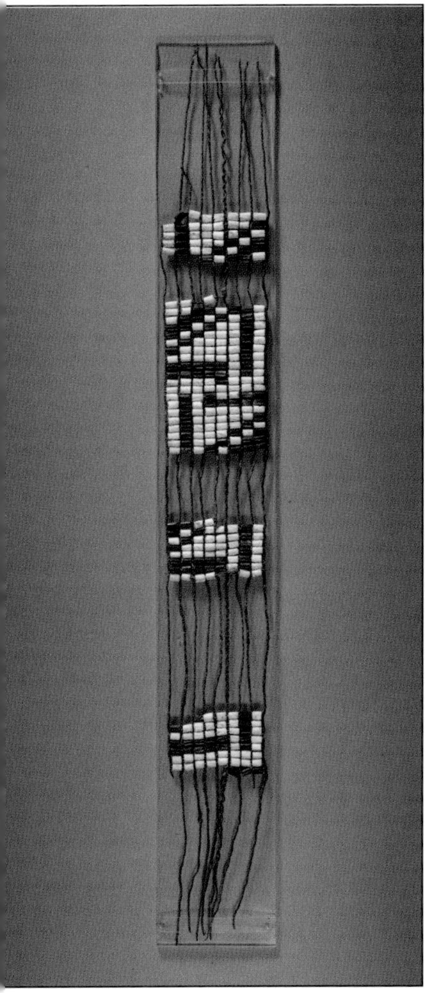

This is an example of an Algonquin wampum belt from the 1600s.

the full regal dress of an English gentleman on December 12, 1753. In the middle of a raging snowstorm, he presented a letter written by Dinwiddie that clearly, but politely, asked the French to leave not just the fort but the entire Ohio Valley—or else! Captain Jacques Legardeur de Saint Pierre was the new commander of the fort, and he wrote a reply that was diplomatic but made clear that the French had no intention of leaving. He also pointed out that the letter from Dinwiddie was addressed to the Governor of New France, Michel-Ange Duquesne, so the message would have to be passed on to him for official response.

"As to the summons you send me to retire, I do not think myself obliged to obey it," wrote Captain Pierre. "Whatever may be your instructions, mine bring me here by my general's order; and I entreat you, Sir, be assured that I shall attempt to follow them with all the exactness and determination which can be expected of a good officer." The entire business was conducted with utter courtesy, but it was not the reply George Washington had wished for. When Washington left, Half-King Tanacharison and his men stayed on to discuss other matters with the French.

Washington left convinced that the French not only had no intention of leaving, but in all likelihood would be sending more men into the area to build forts. As he made his way back to Williamsburg with the bad news, Washington encountered horrible winter weather. His account of his harrowing journey back east shows how brutal the wilderness could be in winter. He forged many icy streams and rode exhausted horses through heavy snows. When confronted with an ice-filled Allegheny, George Washington and his guide Christopher Gist took out an axe and constructed a log raft. Although they made it across, they were sopping wet and their clothing froze solid. Washington published the details of the entire episode from his journal. The tale swayed much public opinion toward the notion of banding together against France.

The Fight for a Vital Fork

Governor Dinwiddie saw the French response from Fort Le Boeuf as an act of aggression. He believed that military response was the only course of action. Shortly into the new year of 1754, he promoted Washington to Lieutenant Colonel, and ordered him to put together a team of men to confront the French on the Ohio River.

In the meantime, Governor Dinwiddie ordered that a fort be built in present-day Pittsburgh, a strategic fork where the Monongahela and Allegheny Rivers meet to form the Ohio River. William Trent, an English fur trader, had already constructed a small trading post there in the 1740s. In spring of 1754, Virginia workers began building their own fort for the British.

Before they could complete the project, a force of 600 French troops swept in on April 16, 1754. They drove off the few dozen colonial laborers and soldiers, capturing Trent's outpost. They then finished the construction according to their own designs—adding a parade ground, a guardhouse, officer's quarters, supply and gun powder storage areas, a hospital, a blacksmith, and a bakery. Under the command of Captain Pierre de Contrecoeur, the new post was named Fort Duquesne, after New France's governor. With this key piece of land in French control, the British were more alarmed than ever.[2]

In the beginning of April, Washington had assembled about 159 men in Williamsburg, Virginia. They were poorly equipped and ill-trained, but ready to follow George Washington on this mission. They slowly made their way toward the new post constructed by Captain Contrecoeur and his men.

Ben Franklin Takes a Stand!

In the 1750s, Benjamin Franklin of Philadelphia was concerned by the French threat. He was a successful publisher, printing the *Pennsylvania Gazette* and *Poor Richard's Almanack*. He knew that the colonies would have to be united to fend them off. On May 9, 1754, as Washington and his men made their way to Fort Duquesne, he published the first American political cartoon. His woodcut drawing showed a writhing snake cut into pieces, each segment representing one of the colonies. The caption read "Join, or Die." The cartoon struck a chord, and other papers published it in order to push for a unified front in efforts against the encroaching French.

The Skirmish That Starts a War

On May 24, 1754, George Washington had arrived at Grand Meadow, within 40 miles (64 km) of Fort Duquesne. Here, he and his men built Fort Necessity, which was really just a storehouse for gunpowder, rum, and flour. From this position, he led a colonial militia in the first skirmish of the French and Indian War in southwestern Pennsylvania. The French at Fort Duquesne had gotten word of Washington's advance and sent out a scouting party to report on any possible approach by the British. Tanacharison's Indians had spotted the French

The "Join, or Die" cartoon created by Benjamin Franklin was first published in 1754. The cartoon would be re-published in 1765 as a call to the colonies to protest increased taxation under the Stamp Act.

scouting party encampment in a deep glen surrounded with rock. Thirty-three French soldiers—the advance team from Fort Duquesne—were encamped beneath some overhanging rocks.

On the morning of May 28, Washington, forty of his men, and a few Indians surrounded the French scouts. The French were just beginning to wake, emerging from bark shelters they had set up to protect themselves from the rain. A shot rang out and the skirmish begun. In about fifteen minutes, fourteen French soldiers had died in the battle. The surviving French surrendered and threw down their muskets. Washington lost only a single man. He reported that the Indians were particularly savage, killing several of the wounded and scalping them.

Among the wounded was the French group leader, Coulon de Villiers, Sieur de Jumonville. As he lay bleeding, Jumonville was approached by the Half-King Tanacharison. The Indian leader asked if he was English or French. When he replied French, Tanacharison took his tomahawk and split open the head of the wounded de Jumonville. A soldier in Washington's regiment later reported that the Half-King washed his hands in Jumonville's brains and scalped him.[3]

Although he had never seen such barbaric behavior, Washington appreciated the help from the Indians. He wrote later in a letter to Governor Dinwiddie: "There were five or six Indians, who served to knock the poor, unhappy wounded on the head, and bereav'd them of their scalps."

George Washington seemed to enjoy the thrill of battle. He wrote to his brother, "I hear the bullets whistle and believe me, there is something charming in the sound." With this small confrontation, Washington had started a global war.

The surviving captured French insisted that they were on a peaceful diplomatic mission—they were there simply to warn Washington and the British to leave French land. Washington thought it more likely that they were out to spy on British advances. The French and Commander Contrecouer at Fort Duquesne viewed the incident as a massacre of innocent men.

Washington's First Defeat

Reinforcements soon arrived at Fort Necessity, raising the numbers to about 400, and Washington debated whether he should push on to take Fort Duquesne. Holding him back was the knowledge that the French had about 500 trained soldiers. He tried to convince the Delaware, Shawnee, and Iroquois to join his attack on the French, but they refused.

By June 26, more French soldiers and a group of about 125 Indians arrived at Fort Duquesne bringing French forces up to 1,000. Set on revenge, Captain Coulon de Villiers (the brother of the leader who died in Washington's initial attack) traveled up the Monongahela River toward Fort Necessity early on July 3, 1754. Washington was no match for such numbers. The French killed all of Washington's horses and livestock. His regiment struggled as many of their guns jammed and their gunpowder was wet. In a short time, a third of Washington's men were dead or wounded. Some surviving soldiers decided to get drunk on the rum provisions instead of fighting. On July 4, a day that would later hold so much importance in American history, Washington surrendered. He sent van Braam out with a white flag. De Villiers sent van Braam back with a rain-soaked paper detailing the terms of the truce. [4]

Although the agreement was difficult to read, van Braam translated the French the best he could. Washington agreed to the terms. All his men would be allowed to march out with the honors of war and keep their arms. Soldiers captured by Washington in the May 28th skirmish were to be returned, but De Villiers demanded two hostages. Van Braam and another commander, Robert Stobo, volunteered. Washington had to vow to stay out of the Ohio Valley for just over a year.

Not fully understanding the French in the surrender agreement, Washington unknowingly signed an agreement stating that he had assassinated Sieur de Jumonville. The French would now brand Washington as a villain and use this episode to justify their expansion in Ohio. With the French now dominating the area, Indians who sided with the French made raids on English settlements. As Washington and his troops retreated, the French destroyed Fort Necessity and many of his troops deserted.

Washington made his way to Williamsburg by July 17, and told Dinwiddie about the dismal defeat. Although Dinwiddie was determined to regroup and push back against the French, he did not fully trust that Washington was seasoned enough to be a military commander. Dinwiddie decided on a new approach and broke up Washington's regiment into independent companies of soldiers led by captains. For Washington, this meant a demotion, so he resigned in October of 1754 and concentrated on building his farm at Mount Vernon.

4

A STORM ON THE HORIZON

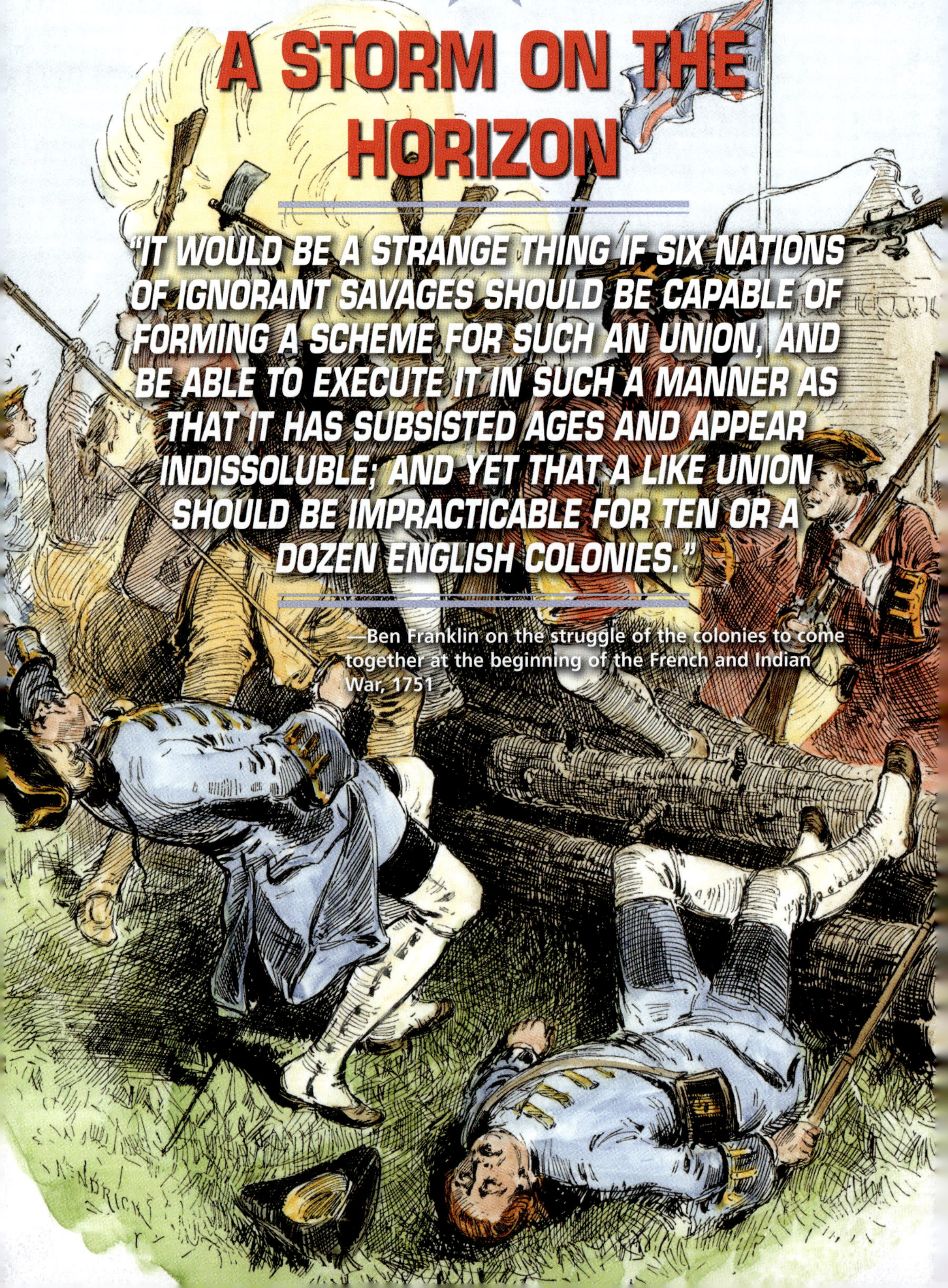

"IT WOULD BE A STRANGE THING IF SIX NATIONS OF IGNORANT SAVAGES SHOULD BE CAPABLE OF FORMING A SCHEME FOR SUCH AN UNION, AND BE ABLE TO EXECUTE IT IN SUCH A MANNER AS THAT IT HAS SUBSISTED AGES AND APPEAR INDISSOLUBLE; AND YET THAT A LIKE UNION SHOULD BE IMPRACTICABLE FOR TEN OR A DOZEN ENGLISH COLONIES."

—Ben Franklin on the struggle of the colonies to come together at the beginning of the French and Indian War, 1751

In June and July of 1754, representatives from seven of the thirteen English colonies gathered in Albany New York for what became known as the Conference of Albany.[1] Alliances among the English settlements were not new. In the mid-1600s, Massachusetts Bay, Plymouth, Connecticut, and New Haven had come together and formed the New England Confederation. They were able to negotiate terms with the Dutch settlers and avoid conflict. Colonies also came together during King Philip's War, Queen Anne's War, and King George's War.

At this 1754 gathering, representatives of the Iroquois Confederacy were also in attendance. The goal of the colonies was to discuss how to improve relations with the Indians and what measures they could take to fend off the French. The alliances and treaties set up between the English and the Indians were known collectively as The Covenant Chain, and they had begun as early as the 1670s. The meeting was a sign of greater unity for the colonies, but Connecticut, Maryland, Massachusetts, New Hampshire, New York, Pennsylvania, and Rhode Island could not agree to any official confederation—they each guarded their independence. The British Crown was wary of such a union as well. Governor Shirley of Massachusetts, however, described their collective work as a general league of friendship, and it did set in motion a movement toward greater unity; this unity would be

Tiyanoka, called Hendrick by the British, is shown wearing a European style military uniform. He helped negotiate peace between the Iroquois Confederacy and the colonies at the Albany Conference in 1754.

essential for the success of the American Revolution years later.

During the conference, the Indians expressed their displeasure with British expansion. Some delegates from the colonies, who had difficulties cooperating, struck their own private deals with the Indians. Connecticut secretly purchased acres that Pennsylvania also had laid claim to. After the Iroquois left with 30 wagons of presents, Benjamin Franklin commented that their Iroquois Confederacy appeared to be more unified and effective than the colonies.

The delegates finally agreed to form a plan of Union of the Colonies by Act of Parliament. They wanted this Union to be approved by British parliament, and make sure that the royal crown would help pay for war measures going forward. When the delegates all left Albany for home on July 11, 1754, they had copies of the Albany Plan for Union. In many regards, this document would become the foundation for the U.S. Constitution some 30 years later. The colonial legislatures, however, could not get behind the Albany Plan and it was rejected. The colonies were still too interested in their own self-interests to sign up.

The Conflict Heats Up

The following year, although there had been no formal declaration of war between France and Britain, the war in North America had already begun. The British plotted to take Fort

Duquesne, Fort Niagara, Fort Saint-Frédéric on Lake Champlain, and Fort Louisbourg in Nova Scotia, which they had briefly controlled in 1745. In British eyes, they were simply taking back lands that were rightfully theirs. Plus, in Nova Scotia, the British were becoming more wary of the French farmers and fishermen who peacefully settled there. Known as Acadians, these French settlers had been marrying among the Mi`kmaq and Abenaki Indians, establishing closer ties with the natives.

By the summer of 1755, the clouds of a declared war were drawing closer. The French sent ships of reinforcements to Canada. In response England sent eleven ships and two frigates to cruise the waters around Louisbourg and stop them. The British were able to stop a couple French vessels, but many slipped through the fog on the St. Lawrence and continued on to Quebec, bringing thousands of new soldiers to fight at Fort Duquesne and elsewhere.

Braddock Leads the Charge

Still stung by Washington's defeat at Fort Necessity, King George II sent Major General Edward Braddock to the colonies with two regiments of infantrymen. Arriving in February of 1755 in Virginia, the 60-year-old Braddock was overweight and short-tempered.[2] He also had very little experience leading combat of any kind, but he strictly followed British military rules and regulations, and was well-versed in the European style of warfare. When he arrived, the rude, arrogant taskmaster Braddock began giving orders to the colonials and almost immediately created a bad impression. To his credit, though, he was courageous and ready to lead men into battle, no matter the cost.

Despite Braddock's disagreeable nature, George Washington was eager to serve under him. He saw Braddock's arrival as an opportunity to become a professional British officer and develop a career in the regular British army. Knowing that Washington was very familiar with the Ohio wilderness, Braddock hired him as an aide. He promised Washington that he would use his influence to get him a desirable position. Ironically, in twenty years time, Washington would be fighting a war against the British army he had so much wanted to join.

Braddock's primary target was Fort Duquesne, but he also was organizing men to take Fort Frédéric on Lake Champlain in New York, Fort Niagara in New York, and Fort Beauséjour. By now, Fort Duquesne, in the desirable fork where the Monongahela and Allegheny rivers met, was well-protected with cannons and soldiers. It was still the most coveted and symbolic prize for the colonies at the time.

Heading toward battle, Braddock thought he held an advantage: One of the prisoners taken at Washington's defeat at Fort Necessity—Major

Robert Stobo—had been kept at Fort Duquesne. He had made sketches of the fort, which would now help in a British attack.

Expulsion of the Acadians

In May and June of 1755, as Braddock was preparing to set off, other colonial troops had success to the north. On June 16, 2,000 militiamen were able to capture Fort Beauséjour in Nova Scotia. Now that they controlled most of Nova Scotia, the British asked the French Acadians to swear allegiance to the English king or be expelled. The Acadians refused, saying that if they swore allegiance to the English king the French would send Indians to attack their communities and kill them. Also, swearing allegiance to Protestant England would be against their Roman Catholic faith.

The British decided that all the French, who had been settling in this region since the early 1600s, would have to leave. On July 28, 1755, Charles Lawrence, the British governor of "Acadie" ordered what many call the "The Great Upheaval" or "Great Expulsion."[3] As the British burned down homes and farms, the Acadians (numbering about 14,000) were dispersed throughout the colonies on the Eastern Coast. Some families were split up, and many under 21 years of age were made servants to the British colonialists. After the war, many French were sent to the French Caribbean (Antilles,

The Acadians were forced to leave their homes by the British. Here you can see them with their belongings boarding ships. There are flames in the background as the British burn their towns.

Martinique, Saint-Domingue), while others went back to France. Many more Acadians made their way to Louisiana, where they became known as Cajuns (the word comes from Acadian, pronounced 'a-cay-DJYEN' in French). Henry Wadsworth Longfellow made the expulsion of the Acadians famous in his poem *Evangeline, A Tale of Acadie,* the story of a woman in search of her long-lost love, Gabriel. Today, some have described the expulsion of these people to a type of ethnic cleansing.

On June 10, 1755, Braddock set out from Fort Cumberland, Maryland, with 2,000 regulars (British foot soldiers), locals, and sailors to fire heavy cannons that had been unloaded from ships. The troops had almost zero help from the Indians, and that might have made a huge difference. As they headed along Nemacolin's Path (an ancient Native American trail that crossed the Allegheny Mountains), Braddock's men widened it, cutting down trees along the way to make room for the wagons loaded with heavy artillery. They trudged along at a glacial pace of about 3 miles (5 km) a day, constructing bridges over swamps and rivers, and chopping out a 12-foot (3.6 m) wide thoroughfare that would become known as Braddock's Road. Finally, after twenty-two days, Braddock's plodding team reached a point on the east back of the Monongahela River, just 8 miles (13 km) from Fort Duquesne.

On July 8, the British soldiers ate a hearty meal and were full of optimism. They thought they had the military might and skill to handily topple Fort Duquesne. The next day, as Braddock launched his attack, Washington was in poor shape, suffering from dysentery (an infection in the intestines that causes severe diarrhea). Washington could only ride his horse by tying cushions to the saddle. But there he was, just over a year after his surrender at Fort Necessity, heading into battle.

The French, under the leadership of Contrecoeur, were not going to wait for the British to march up to their fort and begin pummeling it with artillery fire. So as the British moved closer to Fort Duquesne, the French sent out a battalion of soldiers and Indians led by Captain Daniel Liénard de Beaujeu. He was well-respected by the French and Indians alike. And Beaujeu had a large number of fearsome warriors on his side, including Ottawas, Mississaugas, Wyandots, and Potawatomis. When the two opposing forces confronted each other, Beaujeu gave a signal for the Indians to go into the woods and surround the oncoming British from the sides.

Despite the British outnumbering the French forces by almost two to one, the British made themselves an easy target. Although Washington warned Braddock that the French and Indian fighting style was not at all like the conventions

Braddock was mortally wounded during the fighting near Fort Duquesne. He died several days later.

of European warfare, Braddock had followed the old-school approach to battle engagement. He lined up his men in columns and marched them forward, dressed in their easy-to-spot bright red uniform coats.

Despite a chance bullet killing Beaujeu early in the siege, the French dominated. The French and their Indian allies shot at them with arrows and guns from behind the bushes. Scalping the wounded and living alike, the wild, whooping Indians sent icy fingers of fear into the hearts of the British.

Braddock had five different horses shot out from under him, and then he too was mortally wounded by a bullet that penetrated one of his lungs. (Some say the shot might have come from one of his own disoriented men). George Washington narrowly escaped death himself when a bullet took off his hat and his horse was shot. He later wrote to his brother: "I had four bullets through my Coat, and two horse shot under me, and yet escaped unharmed."

Mayhem spread through the British-led ranks. Some of the local colonials who were fighting took cover in the bushes, just as the French had. This confused the British and they shot at those colonials as well. They killed some of their own troops, mistaking them for the enemy. With Braddock mortally wounded, Washington helped lead the British in retreat. It was a less than spectacular start to his military career.

According to some accounts, the British lost 977 men to the French's nine. When he died on July 14, Braddock was buried under the road he had cut. Walter Borneman wrote in his book, The French & Indian War, that a long stretch of bleached bones from the British colonialists could be seen five years later. The bones were spread "so thick that one lies on top of another for about a half mile in length, and about 100 yards in breadth."[4]

The Indians celebrated their take of supplies, weapons, scalps, and prisoners. They tortured and burned prisoners at the stake. The French also had captured wagons, weapons, ammunition, and the general's trunk. Inside this container, the French found crucial plans for attacks on Fort Niagara and Fort Frédéric. That year, 1755, an army under the leadership of Governor William Shirley of Massachusetts failed to reach Fort Niagara. He decided to leave 700 of his men to strengthen their base at Fort Oswego on the southeast shore of Lake Ontario.

Because the French found British war plans in Braddock's chest, they were able to head off the plans to attack Fort Frédéric. Before the British could launch their assault from Fort Edward just south of Lake George on the Hudson River, the French tried to strike. On September 8, 1755, about 1,500 British forces met 1,500 French troops at the Battle of Lake George. In the end, the bloody confrontation was considered a victory for the British. In Mohawk history, however, it is seen as a dark day. Different Mohawk groups allied themselves with either British or French forces. Fellow Indians wound up fighting their brothers to the death in hand-to-hand combat. In the end, the British secured the southern end of Lake George and build Fort William Henry, completing it on November 13, 1755.

When the British lost Mohawk allies after this battle, Governor Shirley put together companies of rangers who acted as scouts and raiders. The rangers were locals who were familiar with frontier combat. They used Indian tactics of secrecy, ambush, and surprise. From time to time, they would sack, burn, and destroy French settlements. Under the command of Major Robert Rogers, the rangers in the Lake George and Lake Champlain region would get around by skating and snowshoeing. Rogers' Rangers became famous for their effectiveness and unconventional methods. British commander-in-chief Loudoun said that it was

Losses were heavy on both sides of the Battle of Lake George. In the end, victory went to the British.

impossible for an army to act in America without Rangers.[5]

As the colder months of winter approached in 1755, both sides took a pause to regroup and strategize. The French and Indians realized that they had the upper hand in the Ohio Valley at this point and they conducted many small raids on advancing colonial settlements.

Seeing that Washington had gained respect and experience, Governor Dinwiddie promoted Washington to be the commander-in-chief of all Virginia forces. He spent time touring the devastated frontier settlements, trying to get support from the Indians and attempting to bring order and discipline to the troops at Fort Cumberland (a British outpost on the frontier in

Maryland). He was highly discouraged, not only by the encroaching French, but also by conflicts with British command and troops that were unruly and frequently drunk. Yet, for all the hardships, Washington gained invaluable experience and knowledge of the American landscape, which would serve him well in the American Revolution.

Demoralized after this latest massive defeat at Fort Duquesne, the British forces spiraled down into a three-year period known as the "years of losing."

The War Officially Begins

While the French and Indian War had effectively started with George Washington's 1754 attack near Fort Necessity, France and Britain had not yet officially declared war. However, it was on the horizon. After the War of the Austrian Succession ended in 1748, Prussia retained control of the Austrian territory of Silesia. Maria Theresa, Queen of Austria, desperately wanted to take back Silesia. As Frederick the Great, King of Prussia gained power, Austria joined forces with Sweden and France to oppose Prussia. They would later be joined by Russia and Spain. England sided with Prussia.

In April of 1756, France beefed up its forces in Canada, sending in new troops and a new leader, the very capable General Louis-Joseph Montcalm. To retaliate for the 1755 attacks in North

America, France decided to launch a decisive blow by taking the British Island of Minorca (sometimes spelled Menorca)-Britain's main naval base in the Mediterranean. When France invaded the island, Britain officially declared war on May 15, 1756.[6] The Seven Years' War (known as the French and Indian War in America) had officially begun. To escalate matters, on August 29, 1756, Prussia invaded Austria's ally, Saxony, and then proceeded on to Bohemia. The French and British were also tangling for territory in India, so resources on all sides were stretched to the limit.

In 1755 the British had started attacks on the French. In the spring of 1756, with the two nations officially at war, the French decided it was its turn to launch a counter assault. Montcalm coordinated the offensive but acted according to the wishes of the Governor of New France, Marquis de Vaudreuil.

5

THE SHIFTING BALANCE OF POWER

"I AM SURE THAT I CAN SAVE THIS COUNTRY, AND NOBODY ELSE CAN."

—William Pitt, secretary of state in England, during the French and Indian War, 1756

The Governor of New France, Vaudreuil, and the leader of military forces, Montcalm, did not often get along.[1] Vaudreuil had already accepted the effectiveness of using Indian fighters and guerrilla tactics—raids that resembled hunting parties. Montcalm still favored more traditional European military tactics, but learned to incorporate Indians in his sieges. The two both saw themselves as leaders in New France, and they butted heads. By most accounts, Vaudreuil was vain and egotistical. He became jealous of the Montcalm's successes.

To be fair, Montcalm's victories were often due to Vaudreuil's planning, but Vaudreuil felt he received little of the credit. He grew to see Montcalm as a rival. Montcalm was known for his quick temper. This rivalry and animosity between Montcalm and Vaudreuil would eventually contribute to the downfall of New France.

There was one other person in the mix who weakened New France: Francois Bigot.[2] He was called the Intendant of New France and controlled the entire civil administration, the justice system, and all finances. He was also entirely corrupt. He set up an elaborate system of fraud whereby each branch of public service had to pay him a fee. His scheme made him and his cronies rich, but the corruption helped speed the collapse of the new French empire.

Montcalm fought in the War of the Polish Succession and the War of the Austrian Succession before he was sent to New France to take charge of the troops there.

Montcalm Remains Calm.... and Victorious

Despite his flaws, Montcalm was a strong military leader,

and his initial sieges began with success. As in the British colonies, his military force consisted of regulars (soldiers who came directly from France to fight), Canadian militiamen (locals from Canada who were trained for battle), and sometimes Indians. The regulars often viewed themselves as superior to the militiamen and treated them shabbily. Although Montcalm too felt that militiamen did not have the discipline of his regular soldiers, he gained their confidence and used them effectively.

He also learned to work with the Indians, but wrote that it required great patience to get along with them. Like Washington, he was taken aback by their outbursts of savagery. According to the 1902 book *Montcalm and Wolfe* by Francis Parkman, Montcalm said: "They make war with astounding cruelty, sparing neither men, women, or children, and take off your scalp very neatly—an operation which generally kills you."

Along Lake Ontario, the British had now had put up a complex of defenses consisting of Fort Oswego, Fort Ontario, and Fort George. The French learned, however, that the British forces here were struggling; many of their men were suffering from scurvy and a lack of food. Montcalm decided to strike while the enemy was down. In the summer of 1756, using 200 flat-bottomed boats called *bateaux*, General Montcalm coordinated 3,000 men to sail from their Fort Frontenac (in today's Kingston,

Canada) and discreetly edge along the coast of Lake Ontario toward the British Fort Oswego.

On August 12, 1756, the French began their bombardment of the fort with a line of cannon fire. Lieutenant Colonel James Mercer, the commander at Oswego, and his men were no match for the massive force. He and his men evacuated to nearby Fort Ontario, but Montcalm's siege was unrelenting, and he took all three forts. Colonel Mercer fell dead, beheaded by an incoming cannonball.[3] After the British surrendered, Montcalm burned Fort Oswego to the ground and boasted of dominating an area crucial to British trade.

He reported taking 1,600 prisoners, five flags, one hundred guns, two hundred bateaux, and "an astonishing booty made by our Canadians and Indians." England and the colonies were shaken. At this point, the French appeared to be winning the war not only in North America but on a global scale as well. They had already taken Minorca in the Mediterranean and their allies had defeated the forces of Fort William in Calcutta, India.

As France Rises, England Finds a Savior

While King George II ruled England, the country also had a parliament that guided most government decisions and was led by a prime minister. Thomas Pelham-Holles, the duke of Newcastle, was prime minister as the French and Indian War began. It was obvious, however, that England needed new leadership during this time of war. William Pitt, with his immense ego, assertiveness, and love of country, was the man for the occasion. Pitt could not get enough support to become prime minister, but Newcastle saw that he was needed to lead the war effort. Newcastle named Pitt secretary of state in 1756. For a brief interlude between November 16, 1756, and June 25, 1757, The Duke of Devonshire replaced Newcastle as prime minister, but then Newcastle returned to form a fruitful partnership with Pitt and a new government.

Pitt butted heads with King George II but was popular among the people. Newcastle, on the other hand, had good relations with the monarchy. Newcastle and Pitt did not always get along well, but by working together these two opposite forces had what was needed to guide England in the right direction. Pitt conducted the war effort, while Newcastle soothed the king. Pitt boldly declared, "I am sure that I can save this country, and nobody else can."[4]

In 1757, New France was holding the upper hand in North America, but there were weaknesses in the approach from the mother country. France wasn't as tied to the sea as England; it saw its greatest strength in a strong army. So the country devoted more resources to its army than it did to its navy. Plus, France was

William Pitt the Elder's bold leadership helped end the French and Indian War and gained Britain a vast empire.

not as interested in the backwoods of North America as it was in the territories it might control in Europe. So while France directed 100,000 men into battle in Austria, it only sent a few thousand now and then to New France. This imbalance would cost France in the end.

A British Step Forward and Back Again

The fighting was at a standstill in the winter of 1756–57. Montcalm and his government of New France were enjoying themselves after a string of successes by entertaining guests who had traveled from Europe to celebrate with them. Pitt and the British colonial forces, meanwhile, were determining the most effective attack against the French. The new plan was to attack the problem at its head and take out Quebec, which was the capital of New France. To do so, the English would first need to cut off French access to the St. Lawrence River by seizing Fort Louisbourg, which was still under French control.

After Braddock died, England sent John Campbell, known as Lord Loudoun, to take his place. He became Governor of Virginia and supreme commander of all British forces in North America. As with Braddock, the colonists found Loudoun difficult to get along with.[5] Loudoun had a sense of arrogance and superiority toward the colonists that seemed common among the British. Political decisions went through each colony's governor and its elected body or assembly. When the Virginia assembly opposed decisions by Loudoun, he would threaten to use force against them. This attitude fueled a growing resentment against the Crown.

Despite conflict with the colonists, Lord Loudoun organized a siege of Fort Louisbourg on Cape Breton Island at the mouth of the St. Lawrence. Early in the summer of 1757, he pulled many men from New York to prepare for battle in Nova Scotia. On June 20, Lord Loudoun left New York with a fleet of 100 ships carrying 6,000 men. Britain also sent Vice Admiral Francis Holburne and his fleet, which sailed from Ireland with 5,000 more men. The two fleets met in Halifax, Nova Scotia on July 7 and planned their assault on Fort Louisbourg. In the meantime, the 74-year-old French Admiral Dubois de La Motte arrived at Louisbourg with 20 warships. Now, the French had an estimated 9,000 soldiers and 1,200

Indians. Seeing that France had put together such a strong defense, Loudoun determined that a successful siege was impossible and turned back to New York in the beginning of August.

A Massacre on Lake George

As Loudoun had taken soldiers from New York for his Louisbourg plan, Montcalm figured it was an opportune moment to assail Fort William Henry, a British outpost on the southern end of Lake George. Montcalm began assembling thousands of troops at Fort Carillon, just north of Lake George and 15 miles (24 km) south of Fort Saint-Frédéric on Lake Champlain. With about 6,000 soldiers and 1,800 Indians, Montcalm descended on Fort William Henry, where there were only about 2,000 defenders.

The French floated bateaux filled with large artillery and troops down Lake George. About 15 miles (24 km) south, more soldiers were stationed at Fort Edward, but the British military leaders decided it would be more important to keep Fort Edward well-fortified than send soldiers from there into battle.

On August 2, 1757, with cannons positioned within a half mile of Fort William Henry, the French started a seven-day bombardment. On August 9, commander Colonel Monro surrendered. Representatives met in a courteous manner, according to the European rules of warfare and conditions were settled upon. The

British and their followers agreed not to fight for a period of eighteen months. The French would take Fort William Henry and then provide safe escort of the conquered to Fort Edward. The British could keep their personal items, guns, and one cannon that represented their brave defense. The French would attend to the sick and wounded at Fort William Henry until they recovered. All in all, it was a very civil arrangement.

Although Montcalm said that he had explained the terms of surrender to the Indians, they did not understand, or simply would not accept them. They were determined to get compensation by taking booty, prisoners, and scalps. On that day of August 10, the first major group of captives was taken on the journey toward Fort Edward. It all should have been a peaceful process. Giving no regard to the agreement, however, the Indians descended on the British. They killed and scalped many, taking their possessions. Sometimes, they captured women and children. Some records show that upwards of 185 British were murdered and scalped, and three to five hundred were taken prisoners. (This brutal episode in history is depicted in James Fenimore Cooper's novel, *The Last of the Mohicans.*)[6]

The Indians gave the same brutal treatment to the sick and wounded left in the fort hospital. Little did they know, that many of the sick were infected with small pox, and their clothes also carried the virus. This disease would eventually kill thousands of Indians. After taking this critical British fort, Montcalm should have felt the joy of victory, but the massacre had deprived the French of some glory. Both sides felt that the raid had been an atrocity. Rather than try to man the fort, Montcalm ordered it to be burned.

The episode also soured relations between the French and the Indians. Many Indians felt that Montcalm had deceived them because they were not given outright the spoils of war that they felt should have been theirs. For the British colonists, the floodgates of outrage had broken open and they were more determined than ever to win. In Europe, England was not faring any better, surrendering Hanover in Germany to France.

This engraving shows the brutality of the Native American attack on the British captives.

The Tide Turns With Pitt

By the spring of 1758, Secretary of State Pitt in England was undaunted. He committed more men, ships, and money to the war in North America. He didn't like how the former British leaders in North America interacted with the colonists. He reached out to the governors and assemblies with an offer to work closely together to build a larger military force. Pitt vowed that he would urge Parliament to reimburse the colonies for the costs of feeding, training, and maintaining new recruits. Colonists could now also achieve ranks equal to those of the British officers. All these concessions gave the colonists more incentive to work together with the British to defeat the French.

Pitt was determined to aggressively attack New France. Even far away on the European front, he knew he could aid them by employing the Royal Navy to block French ships heading west with soldiers and supplies.

New France, on the other hand, was beginning to have cracks in its armor. In addition to the mother country not sending sufficient support, crop failures and food shortages were plaguing Canada in 1758.

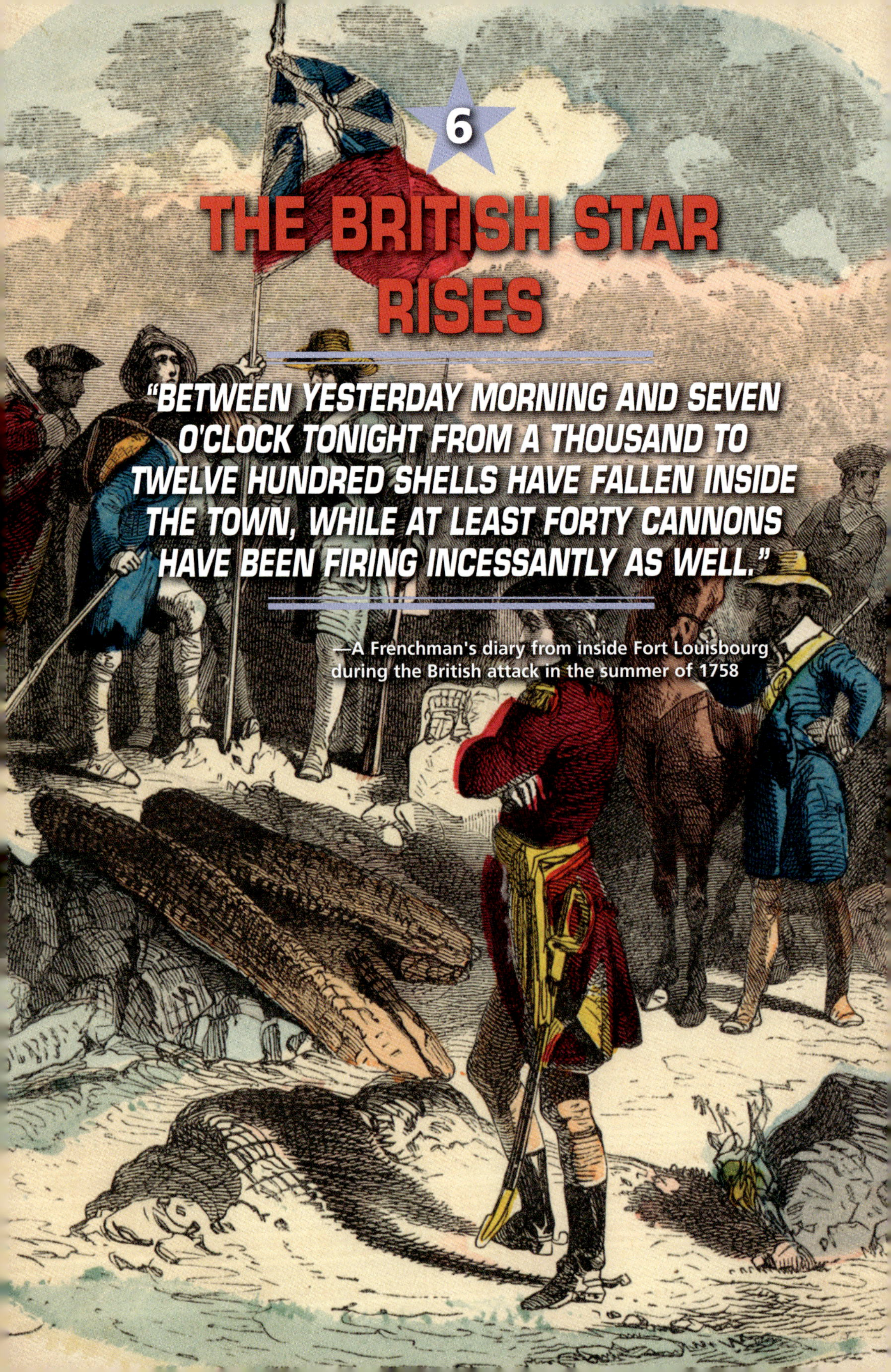

6

THE BRITISH STAR RISES

"BETWEEN YESTERDAY MORNING AND SEVEN O'CLOCK TONIGHT FROM A THOUSAND TO TWELVE HUNDRED SHELLS HAVE FALLEN INSIDE THE TOWN, WHILE AT LEAST FORTY CANNONS HAVE BEEN FIRING INCESSANTLY AS WELL."

—A Frenchman's diary from inside Fort Louisbourg during the British attack in the summer of 1758

Pitt first planned a siege of three familiar targets: Fort Louisbourg, Fort Duquesne, and Fort Carillon (on Lake Champlain). Pitt assigned Major General Jeffrey Amherst as commander to seize the fortress at Louisbourg, with his second in command General James Wolfe. The naval operations under Admiral Edward Boscawen.[1] In June 1758, a force of about 14,000 British fighters boarded boats sailing toward Louisbourg. Only about 3,000 French were stationed there under the command of Chevalier de Drucour. Although the British had successfully blocked many ships heading to Canada, a few got through, so Louisbourg had the additional support of about 3,500 sailors.

The British moved steadily and aggressively. They surrounded the fort by June 19 and commenced artillery fire. War was a horrible affair, but there could be moments for civilized behavior. Although they were enemies, the leaders on either side of the battle considered themselves gentlemen, even in the heat of battle. At one point in the fighting, Amherst paused to send a messenger to the fort—specifically to deliver a gift of two pineapples for Drucour's wife Marie-Anne and a note apologizing for the inconvenience that the siege must be causing on her home. In appreciation, Drucour sent back several bottles of champagne.[2] In a later exchange, the English sent more pineapples to the French, who sent a gift of homemade butter in return. Monsieur Drucour also offered the services of French surgeons to wounded English officers.

All pleasantries aside, Fort Louisbourg was pummeled for 49 days. Drucour foresaw that the British would want to go on to Quebec, so he held them off as long as possible. The closer it got to the colder days of fall and winter, the harder it would be to move on and attack Quebec. A winter delay might give the French time to better defend itself in other locations.

Many of the British hungered for revenge after the massacre at Fort William Henry. Finally, Fort Louisbourg fell to the British on July 26, 1758. They left Louisbourg in ruins with the largest and best buildings all reduced to rubble. The fighting, fortunately, ended before many civilians were harmed. The French soldiers were taken as prisoners and none were awarded the "honors of war"—they gave up all arms, equipment, and flags. French officers were allowed to keep only their swords.

As in Nova Scotia, the British decided that the best protection for Cape Breton Island would be to deport all 8,000 residents to France.[3] The French fleet at Louisbourg was destroyed and access down the St. Lawrence was now almost impossible for the French. The French outposts began to fall like dominoes. Through the remainder of 1758, the English pushed on to take over French settlements in New Brunswick, Prince Edward Island, and Newfoundland. Although the English had a long way to go, the war was now turning decisively in their favor.

A Last Clever Win for Montcalm

Although the British were beginning to dominate the French and Indian War, the British would have to suffer one more major loss before surging ahead. In July 1758, the British were advancing on Fort Carillon. The charge was led by Major General James Abercromby, commander-in-chief of the British forces in North America. Abercromby, however, was unlike the

This engraving shows Abercromby's advance up Lake George before the Battle of Carillon.

energetic General Amherst. He was slow to action, almost overthinking every move. Fortunately, Abercromby had the very able Brigadier Lord William Howe at his side. Considered a very effective leader, Abercromby's second-in-command instilled confidence in all the men. About 15,000 troops were assembling in Albany, New York, for a push north. Montcalm was severely outnumbered with just about 3,500 men at Fort Carillon.[4]

Gathering at the southern end of Lake George in New York on July 5, near the remnants of Fort William Henry, the British and colonial soldiers boarded 900 bateaux and 125 whaleboats. The huge force of men and weapons sailing north stretched almost the entire width of the lake, and for anyone witnessing the advance, it must have been an amazing site.

On July 6, they came ashore at the north end of the lake. French Fort Carillon, on the south end of Lake Champlain, stood about 4 miles (6.4 km) away. As Howe led the men forward, they entered a firefight with an advance group of French soldiers. The British were able to stop these troops, killing 300 and taking 148 prisoners. In the conflict, however, Howe was struck dead by a musket ball. Without their strong guiding leader, the British troops fell into confusion and retreated to their encampment on Lake George.

Things looked promising for the British here. Montcalm was facing a powerful force and feared defeat, but he tried to make the most of the resources he had. The French troops hurried to construct trenches and log walls with holes for guns. They enforced the structures with sandbags. Montcalm camouflaged the entrenchments with fir trees and shrubs. In front of these walls, the French placed *abatis,* a massive tangle of felled trees with sharpened branches intended to slow the advance of the British. The word *abatis* is related to the French word *abattoir*, meaning slaughterhouse.

An inexperienced British engineer, Lieutenant Matthew Clerk, observed the French activities and reported that the fortifications appeared to be insignificant and easy to breach. Based on this

This engraving shows what an abatis looks like.

intelligence, Abercromby ordered a frontal assault on Fort Carillon on July 8. The men were to move swiftly forward and return any enemy fire coming from the trenches. As the British marched in orderly fashion directly toward the enemy, they fell into disorganization when they encountered the maze of fallen trees and sharp branches. The *abatis* certainly proved to be a slaughterhouse as the French mercilessly shot the British down from their trenches, killing or wounding as many as 2,000. The French lost just 106, with 266 wounded—yet their total number of soldiers at this battle had been one fifth that of the British forces.

Ordering a retreat, Abercromby led his men hurriedly back down Lake George to the remains of Fort William Henry. Montcalm celebrated as the largest British army ever put together on American soil fled in defeat.

The British Keep Coming

As discouraging as this defeat was, the British would not quit that easily. They quickly came up with plans to seize Fort Frontenac, located at a crucial point where the St. Lawrence River leaves Lake Ontario. Frontenac had grown into a major commercial outpost and 85 years had passed without any assaults on it. Capturing Frontenac would block a major artery of business in New France. The French tried to save the post by sending about 4,000 troops from Montreal, but they did not make it there in time. On August 25, 1758, under the leadership of John Bradstreet, 3,000 men easily overtook the 110 men defending it. Still, knowing that such a force was coming, Bradstreet allowed the French men, women, and children in Frontenac to make their way to Montreal. Then he destroyed as much of the fort as possible and made off with the weapons, clothes and provisions from the fort.

Bradstreet hurried back to General Abercromby to get permission to push on and take Fort Niagara. But Abercromby, who was notoriously slow to move, put it off for a year. If they had known that only 40 Frenchmen defended that fortress, they might have made a different decision.[5]

In early September, about 80 miles (129 km) north of Albany at Fort Carillon, Montcalm received news that Louisbourg and Frontenac had fallen. He felt that Governor Vaudreuil was sleeping on the job. Fearing the worst, Montcalm set off for New France.

Back to the Stubborn Thorn

The third prong of Pitt's attack was back at Fort Duquesne where both George Washington and Braddock had ultimately failed. In the Ohio Valley region, the Delaware and Shawnee Indians were aligned with the French. Using Fort Duquesne as a base, these natives hit the British settlers in this region hard. Since Braddock's defeat in 1755, the French and Indians had been successful in pushing the colonists back and extending the French borders farther East. In the summer and into the fall of 1758, the Scotsman John Forbes led the newest British offense on Fort Duquesne. His second in command was Lieutenant Colonel Henry Bouquet, a French Huguenot. He was an example of how the French policy of restricting settlement to just Catholics may have helped lead to their defeat.

Forbes believed in a method of conquering called "protected advance."[6] He wanted to move troops forward and build forts as they went, having locations to fall back on for protection. This line of forts would provide a better chain of supplies and communications to the front lines as well. Instead of using Braddock's Road, Forbes built a new road across Pennsylvania, which became known as Forbes Road.[7] He thought the French would not expect this new route.

Washington, who was also to join this next siege on Fort Duquesne, argued against building a whole new road. He saw it as a waste of time, manpower, and resources, when they already had a perfectly good route, Braddock's Road. When Forbes insisted on building a new road, Washington went over Forbes's head to his superior with his complaint. This further strained the relationship between Washington and his British superiors.

British troops worked most of the summer of 1758 on the new road, which started near Harrisburg, Pennsylvania and stretched 200 miles (322 km) east. Along the way, Forbes built his forts. About 40 miles (64 km) southeast of Fort Duquesne, the British under Bouquet built Fort Ligonier, which became their base for the new assault on Fort Duquesne.

At this time, Fort Duquesne was struggling under the command of Francois-Marie le Marchand de Lignery. His troops ranged from 1,000 to 2,000, but supplies were scarce. His supply lines had been cut from Frontenac and Louisbourg. Lignery did not think he had the manpower to survive a full assault by the British so he decided to initiate a series of raids that he thought would help slow or even push back the

British. If he could last until the challenging rains and snow of fall and winter came, he might have a chance. In September 1758, French-siding Indians launched strikes on the new Fort Ligonier, capturing some soldiers and killing and scalping one.

On the British side, Bouquet received an erroneous report that Fort Duquesne only had 600 men, so he advanced on September 14 with about 750 men. The French presented a furious counterattack that left the British scurrying back to Fort Ligonier in defeat. While the French captured or killed about 300, they only lost eight men in this round. The English feared a repeat of General Braddock's famous loss.

On October 12, the French again decided to take the initiative with a counterattack on Fort Ligonier. About 400 French soldiers and militia descended with 100 Indians. While the Indians made off with most of the British horses, the French were repelled.

October, however, brought an important advantage to the British in the Ohio Valley. Representatives of the Delaware and Ohio Indians and members of the Six Nations agreed to meet with the British in Easton, Pennsylvania, north of Philadelphia. The Iroquois wanted the colonies to give up purchases west of the Allegheny Mountains. They wanted the Ohio Valley reserved as indigenous land. The Iroquois would then be the leaders in the region, but

This engraving shows Washington planting the flag at Fort Duquesne the day after the French burned the Fort and abandoned it to the British.

Pennsylvanians would go directly to the Ohio Indians for local matters.

Believing the British promises, the Indians signed the Easton Treaty on October 25, 1758. The King of England even ratified the treaty. After the French surrender, however, British commanders broke many of their promises to the Indians to abandon French forts and many settlers refused to leave as well.

After signing the Easton Treaty, however, Indian support for the French in this region evaporated. Although the harsher weather of November was now upon them, the British decided to push forward. Despite participating in two failed attempts at taking Fort Duquesne, George Washington was back in the picture as well. On November 12, Forbes sent Washington and 500 men in pursuit of a French party that

Forbes discusses his plans with his officers outside the smoldering Fort Duquesne.

had stolen more horses. Forbes also sent a General Mercer to follow him to give him backup. In a case of friendly fire, Mercer and his men initially mistook Washington's encampment as the enemy's and shot at them. The incident left 35 dead before they realized the mistake. Washington survived the mix-up.

In the French camp, Lignery realized that with so little supplies and no support from the Indians, and with the British parked outside, Fort Duquesne was doomed. He ordered his men to pack all valuables. Then, they set the fort ablaze and left. On November 25, Forbes and Washington saw the smoke in the distance and found nothing but smoldering ruins. They also discovered the dead bodies of their comrades who had failed in their first assault. The Indians had cut off many of their heads and placed them on stakes.

Now the British controlled the crucial point where the Allegheny and Monongahela meet to form the Ohio River. The prize that had eluded them for so long was now theirs. They began rebuilding a new outpost immediately. It would be named Fort Pitt after the English Secretary of State who had guided the British to victory. In time, the city surrounding the fort would become Pittsburgh.

Although the war was not over, it was over for George Washington. Taking Fort Duquesne was a pivotal moment for him. On January 1, 1759, he resigned his command. The 26-year-old married Martha Custis five days later and returned to the farm life at Mount Vernon. He spent the next 16 years in relative peace and calm, only to return to the battlefield as the commander-in-chief of the Continental Army in 1776 during the American Revolution.

7

THE FALL OF NEW FRANCE

"NOW GOD BE PRAISED, I WILL DIE IN PEACE."

—Major General James Wolfe's final words a the British claimed victory in Quebec on September 13, 1759

As hope dwindled for New France, both Montcalm and Governor Vaudreuil agreed on one thing: Peace would be the best solution. But New France and the colonies could not arrive at their peace terms alone. They needed England and France to come to terms. In New France that winter, the two argued about best next steps. Montcalm wanted to focus on controlling the St. Lawrence while Vandreuil wanted to reestablish Fort Frontenac and reinforce Fort Niagara. The two were, once again, at odds.

Fort Niagara is in present-day Youngsville, New York. Today it is a state park and museum.

Matters got worse when news arrived from King Louis XV praising Montcalm for his victory at Fort Carillon and making him commander in chief of all military forces in Canada. Now Vandreuil would have to follow Montcalm's orders. Although there was little hope that New France would survive, the French would put up a fight into the fall of 1760.

As fortunes for the British grew brighter, Major General Jeffrey Amherst was promoted just like Montcalm. Amherst replaced Abercromby as commander in chief of all British forces in North America. The next plan of action was to finally take Fort Carillon and push north to Fort Saint-Frédéric. To proceed with these missions, Amherst had to shore up his armies and supplies. Because Pitt had yet to send the promised payments to the colonists, Amherst had to work very hard to convince the colonies that they should continue to fight and give money and supplies in support of British troops. He was able to arrange a large bill of credit and get ample funds to pursue the war effort.

As the spring brought warmer weather, the French kept up a steady barrage of quick disruptive raids between the forts along Forbes Trail. They carried out several attacks, taking supplies, horses and wagons. These were all minor disturbances in the big picture.

The British, of course, were not sitting still. Amherst appointed Colonel John Prideaux to lead the charge on Fort Niagara. (Despite his French name, Prideaux was thoroughly British.) Prideaux formed a new alliance with the Indians from the Treaty of Easton and gained the support of 1,000 Iroquois.[1]

The location of Niagara posed some challenges. The fort sat on a high point of land that jutted out into Lake Ontario on the eastern side of the mouth of the Niagara River. The western side of the river mouth, however, was totally unprotected and would make a perfect perch for bombardment. On July 7, 1759, Prideaux and his men were able to set up guns at this location. About 1,000 yards (914 m) to the east of the fort they dug trenches. Inside Fort Niagara, Commandant Pouchot only had about 500 troops. Having surrounded the fort, Prideaux called for Pouchot's surrender. Pouchot kept silent and secretly sent out messengers to ask for relief forces. Meanwhile, Seneca Indians from Fort Niagara and the Iroquois fought each other. Prideaux had promised the Iroquois that they could plunder the fort, so they continued to side with the British. Pouchot delayed fighting as long as he could, but on July 17, the howitzers began shelling Fort Niagara. The French returned fire over the next few days.

Unfortunately, on July 20, British commander Prideaux was killed by a shell fragment from one of his own guns. Pouchot had held the British off until July 24, when a relief force of about 600 French soldiers and 1,000 Indians arrived. The fresh arrivals, however, marched right into a trap. The British had set up an abatis just like the French had done at Fort Carillon. The result this time was a slaughter of the French. The next day, Pouchot surrendered the fort to the British. He and his men were taken as prisoners of war and sent to Albany.

At the end of July, determined not to accept defeat as Abercromby had done at Fort Carillon, Amherst built up a force of 11,000 to again attempt a siege.[2] The French, however, were now so severely weakened that they were quickly withdrawing their forces back to Canada to mount a defense there. On July 26, the approaching British troops heard a huge explosion—the French blew up Fort Carillon and fled to Fort Saint-Frédéric. Amherst swiftly set his men to rebuilding the outpost as Fort Ticonderoga. Pressing on to Fort Frédéric, the British arrived on August 4th and again they found smoldering ruins. Again, Amherst hurried to establish the site as the new Crown Point. Now the French had no major hold in the Ohio Valley or New York. It appeared that the French were falling fast and there was only one more major target now for the English: Quebec.

Pitt had wanted General James Wolfe, who had been part of the successful siege at Louisbourg, to press on to Quebec back in the fall of 1758. Wolfe missed the message as it crossed the Atlantic and instead he headed back to England where he was celebrated for the success of capturing Fort Louisbourg. Wolfe, who was 32, fell in love with a young woman named Katherine Lowther while back in England and they vowed to get married when he returned from his upcoming battle in Quebec.[3] The fiery red-headed Wolfe set sail back to North America on February 14, 1759, with a miniature portrait of his new love as a reminder of her and their expected marriage.

In the spring of 1759, Canada had very little food of its own because of poor harvests and a harsh winter. Fortunately for Montcalm and his troops, 16 French ships managed to sneak by British forces and arrive at Quebec. His 14,000 men were well-fed and re-stocked with ammunitions and other supplies.

With 9,000 official British soldiers, Wolfe led his troops up the Saint Lawrence to the Ile d'Orleans, landing there on June 26.[4] The island in the middle of the seaway is more than twice the size of Manhattan, at 73 square miles (189 sq km). In mid-July, the British had set up a major line of heavy artillery on high ground about .5 miles (.8 km) from Quebec. Quebec was situated in a well-protected position. The city was divided into two sections. The Lower Town, which sat on a narrow strip along the river, had docks, warehouses, and homes. The Upper Town was surrounded by thick stone walls equipped with big guns to ward off any enemy.

Two days after arriving, Wolfe issued a public declaration to the people of Quebec, called Wolfe's Manifesto. He wrote: "The formidable sea and land armament which the people of Canada now behold in the heart of their country is intended by the King, my master, to check the insolence of France, to revenge the insults offered to the British colonies, and totally to deprive the French of their most valuable settlement in North America."

He wrote that Britain had no war to wage with industrious peasants, and he offered them and women and children clemency. He portrayed France as now "inert and incapable." The average citizen could surrender and accept the protection and privileges of the British Crown. The people of Quebec chose to fight.

On July 31, Wolfe ordered an attack, but the French were ready. The British had to fall back after suffering 443 dead or wounded. Wolfe himself was fighting a torturous illness—he had fever, consumption, and other ailments. To treat it, Wolfe was taking opiates and having his blood let, which was a common cure at the time.

Most approaches for attacking Quebec seemed difficult, and one was particularly improbable. Up the river from the city a very steep cliff called l'Anse au Foulon rose to a flat stretch of land called the Plains of Abraham. Getting up l'Anse au Foulon would be a hazardous and difficult task, so when Wolfe sent some troops in that direction Montcalm thought it was just a ruse.

In the dark of the early morning on September 13, 1759, Wolfe guided 4,000 men on flat boats to the bottom of the sheer cliffs of l'Anse au Foulon. The mission seemed like a long shot, but if the British could pull it off, it just might work. French guards heard boats passing in the dark but they assumed they were supply ships from Montreal sneaking by the British, so they were not alarmed by the possibility of attack. When some guards asked "Who goes there?," the British replied "Français." Having made it past French guards, the British soldiers landed and started up the winding narrow path

The Battle on the Plains of Abraham was a pivotal one in the French and Indian War.

to the Plains of Abraham. A small group of Canadian militiamen finally spotted the ascending British and opened fire. A volley of shots ensued, but the British continued. Montcalm could not believe that the British were attacking from this direction, but as daylight broke the shots continued and Montcalm sent troops toward the west of Quebec. By 6 a.m., British soldiers in their bright uniforms were standing two deep, stretched across the entire Plains of Abraham forming what became known as "Wolfe's thin red line."[5]

Alarmed and surprised by this show of force, Montcalm didn't take much time to strategize. He assembled about 3,500 men to face the British line head on. The French advanced and fired at about 150 yards (137 m), but the British waited.

The French advanced again and with 60 yards (55 m) between the two forces, British troops on the sides fired. Then when the French came 20 yards (18 m) closer, the British in the middle fired repeatedly with precision, and then stormed forward in a bayonet charge. Both Wolfe and Montcalm were mortally wounded. The French troops fell into confusion. The battle lasted less than an hour. Although French relief forces, who numbered as many as 5,000, were only miles from Quebec and might have reversed the situation, Quebec surrendered nonetheless. On September 17, 1759, the remaining garrison surrendered and the British flag was raised over the city. The French retreated to their last stronghold, Montreal. Wolfe died at the young age of 32, never to return to his fiancé in England. He continues to be a tragic British hero who stopped the French against difficult odds. Montcalm, who had such a brilliant military career, died before seeing Quebec topple.

While the French were weakened by Quebec's defeat, so were the British. About 7,000 British troops were left behind to control the city of 6,000 frightened Quebec citizens that winter. The British did not take prisoners because they didn't have the resources to handle them. They let the French soldiers return to France and have full military honors. Now the British controlled a city with little food, fuel, or protection. Disease ran rampant. People were dropping from dysentery

Wolfe is surrounded by his officers and a messenger who brings news of the British victory to Wolfe before he dies.

and scurvy. Brigadier James Murray, who was left in charge of the city, said that the harsh weather of 1759 to 1760 left about 1,000 of his men dead and 2,000 more unable to function. Only about 3,000 were capable of fighting.

New France's Last Stand: The Fall of Montreal

Montcalm's successor, General Francois de Lévis, and the Governor Vaudreuil plotted to retake Quebec in the spring when the ice in the St. Lawrence River was clear. On April 20, 1760, the French headed toward Quebec—8,000 strong. On April 28, the British met the French at Sainte-Foy, just west of the city. It was a much bloodier battle than at the Plains of Abraham with 1,100 casualties for the British and 850 for the French. Murray abandoned his artillery and retreated behind the walls of Quebec City. Even in the middle of conflict, however, the two sides showed European military etiquette. Lévis sent General James Murray a basket of spruce boughs upon hearing he liked spruce beer. And Murray sent Lévis a basket of Cheshire cheese.[6]

This would be France's last show of strength in North America, but ultimately they had to retreat. Lévis had been able to get a message to France, telling them of the dire situation and asking for reinforcements. France was able to send off a small convoy with 400 men, but that would hardly make an impact.

When British reinforcements arrived at Quebec in May, the French were forced to retreat to Montreal. In the summer, the British commander Amherst gathered together forces in excess of 10,000 for a massive strike on Montreal. Seeing that the situation was hopeless, Vaudreuil surrendered, signing articles of capitulation on September 8, 1760.[7] These terms stated that Frenchmen and Canadians could freely remain in Canada but they were to be subjects of Great Britain. Those who fought in the war must return to France, however, and vow never to fight in this war again. A week later, the British swiftly took Fort Detroit as well.

When news of Canada's downfall reached France, King Louis XV was reportedly not very concerned. The story goes that news arrived when King Louis XV was meeting with the celebrated author Voltaire, who told the king that it wasn't such a huge issue—"What have we lost—a few acres of snow." Britain, on the other hand, was a celebrating. In England, 1759 became known as *annus mirabilis* or the wonderful year.

With the fall of Montreal in 1760, the bulk of the fighting in the French and Indian War ended. Still, Britain and France were still battling in other parts of the world, so the terms officially ending the war were not yet established. The French offered to make peace, but William Pitt wanted much more territory than the French were ready to give at this point. France especially wanted to maintain its holdings in the Caribbean (where they conducted a lucrative sugar trade) and the Louisiana Territory.

In an attempt to turn French fortunes around, France's King Louis XV turned to his cousin King Charles III of Spain.[8] Charles III disliked Britain for threats it had made against Naples (then controlled by Spain). They were also concerned about such widespread British expansion. On August 15, 1761, the two countries signed the Family Compact of 1761. To seal the deal with Spain, France gave Spain the Island of Minorca in the Mediterranean. The island had spurred the official declaration of the Seven Years' War when France took it from Britain. Spain secretly agreed to declare war on Britain if peace could not be reached by May 1762. Britain, however, found out the terms of the secret Family Pact and declared war on Spain on January 1762. Britain by now was such a well-oiled military machine that Spain would soon regret its decision to go to war with England. Spain quickly suffered losses—giving up ports in Havana, Cuba, and Manila in the Philippines.

As the British were making decisive victories again Spain and France, they also had to deal with a rising problem with Native American groups in the south.

8

THE FINAL STAGES

"MY BROTHERS, WE MUST ALL SWEAR THEIR DESTRUCTION AND WAIT NO LONGER. NOTHING PREVENTS US; THEY ARE FEW IN NUMBERS, AND WE CAN ACCOMPLISH IT."

—Chief Pontiac of the Ottawa tribe rallying a group of Ottawa, Huron and Pottawatomie Indians to destroy the British colonists on May 5, 1763

It would seem that at this point the war was over, but there were still lingering problems. The French maintained outposts in the south on the Alabama and Mississippi Rivers. About 10,000 Cherokee lived in this area. Attakullakulla (whose name translates to "Little Carpenter") was an influential Cherokee leader and the tribe's "First Beloved Man" or tribal chief.[1] Attakullakulla was generally pro-British. In 1730, he had traveled to England as part of a Cherokee delegation.

He rejected the advances of the French, although there were many Cherokee who were pro-French. With the support of several Cherokee leaders, including Mankiller, Old Caesar, and Raven, the French were able to maintain many outposts in Indian territory, including Fort Toulouse near Montgomery, Alabama; Fort Rosalie in Natchez, Mississippi; and Fort St. Pierre in Yazoo, Mississippi.

With the Cherokee as their allies, the British were building forts in Cherokee lands as well, including Fort Prince George near Keowee, South Carolina, and Fort Loudoun in Monroe County, Tennessee. The Cherokee helped the British in a few battles, including General Forbes's attack on Fort Duquesne in 1758. Forbes didn't really appreciate the Cherokee contribution. He thought they were ignorant, lazy savages. In the meantime, attacks between Virginians and Cherokee were growing. Virginia Lieutenant Governor Dinwiddie asked Forbes to send men with Attakullakulla and a delegation of 10 warriors to meet with the Cherokee and tried to salvage relations.

A Rift in Indian Relations

Shortly after Attakullakulla and his team left on November 18, 1758, Forbes stopped them and took their horses and ammunition, declaring them British property. Furious at Forbes, some Indians decided to steal horses from Virginian settlers as they headed home. This outraged the Virginian farmers who sent a posse after the Cherokee. An attack by these farmers left three Cherokee and one farmer dead. Local militia got involved and killed 19 more Cherokee. In retaliation, Cherokee raided settlements, and killed and scalped 19 farmers.

In fall of 1759, Governor William Lyttelton of South Carolina stopped all trade with the Cherokee and on October 5, 1759, he officially declared war on the Cherokee. Lyttelton marched an army of 1,100 to confront them. The Cherokee, however, were desperate for ammunition and supplies, so they decided to negotiate. They sent 29 chiefs to arrange a truce with Lyttelton, but Lyttelton took them all as prisoners at Fort Prince George. Rather than keep the Cherokees in check, the hostage-taking unleashed the Cherokee fury against the British and they raided more settlements.

In February 1760, the Cherokee attacked Fort Prince George attempting to retrieve the hostages. After the Cherokee killed the fort's commander, his second in command ordered the execution of the hostages. In the end, the British prevented the Indians from taking over the fort. The Cherokee also attacked Fort Ninety-Six in South Carolina, but again they did not succeed in overpowering it.

The Cherokee had a few victories—in August 1760 they captured Fort Loudoun in South

Carolina. As the defeated soldiers and families were escorted to Fort Prince George, some Cherokee attacked them killing 32, capturing some, and wounding others. The Cherokee said it was their revenge for the slaughter of the hostages at Fort Prince George.

Ultimately, the British brought in thousands of men who burned down Cherokee villages and farmlands. In the end, Attakullakulla proved again to be a man of peace and negotiated a truce on behalf of the Cherokee, signing a treaty in November 1761. As a result, the Cherokee boundary was pushed farther west. It helped that the confrontational Governor Lyttelton had moved on to a position in the Caribbean and William Bull had become governor. Bull was described as "a native of this province, [and] acquainted with the Indians and their abilities and the interests and affairs of Carolina."[2]

Trade also resumed between the Indians and the Carolinians. Cherokee leaders—Ostenaco, Standing Turkey, and Wood Pigeon—even traveled to London and visited the Tower of London, met the playwright Oliver Goldsmith, drew massive crowds, and had an audience with King George III.

When New France had stopped fighting after the defeat of Montreal. Amherst, who was leader of the British forces in North America, did not have to rely heavily on Indians alliances to fight any more. He therefore established a new policy of not giving presents to the Indians. Giving presents had been a way to show respect and gain trust and allegiance, but now Amherst abolished the practice.

Pontiac's Fight for Native Land

Conflicts with Indian tribes would not totally disappear. Pontiac was the Ottawa Indian chief and an intertribal leader in the Ohio Valley. In 1760, he allowed British troops to pass through Indian lands unmolested. In return, he expected that Indians would be treated with respect. For years, they had lived in relative harmony with the French. They soon realized that the British were not as accommodating as the French. Plus, the British were taking away their hunting grounds and limiting their trade. The Indian's ancestral grounds were swiftly disappearing to British settlements.

As a highly trusted leader among most of the tribes, Pontiac gathered the support of almost every Indian nation from Lake Superior to the lower Mississippi in a plan to expel the British from Indian lands. It became known as Pontiac's Conspiracy or Pontiac's Rebellion.[3] He hoped that if the Indians could be successful, the French might rejoin their fight against the British.

In May of 1763, he coordinated a massive attack from all the tribes—Delaware, Shawnees,

Seneca, Chippewa, Huron, Potawatomi, and Ottawa each launched an assault on the nearest fort and destroyed any nearby undefended settlements. Simultaneously, many British posts fell—in Michigan, New York, Pennsylvania, Maryland, and Virginia. They included Fort Sandusky in Ohio, Fort St. Joseph in Michigan, Fort Miami in Indiana, Fort Presque Isle in Pennsylvania, and Fort Edward Augustus in Wisconsin. The Indians could not take Fort Pitt or Fort Niagara.

Pontiac himself led a sly assault on Fort Detroit that also ultimately failed but inflicted much damage. He arranged a friendly visit with the soldiers, but planned to kill the British once they were inside the fort and the soldiers' guard was down. An Indian girl, however, tipped off Major Gladwyn, commander of Fort Detroit. When Pontiac arrived, he saw that the British were ready for battle and he retreated. Afterward, he and his fellow tribesmen pummeled the fort for months. In June of 1763, British reinforcements came. They thought they'd catch Pontiac's forces off guard at an encampment, but Pontiac got word of their plan and was ready for their push. As 247 British soldiers crossed a small bridge at Parent Creek, Pontiac brought down a savage barrage. The creek ran red with British blood from so much carnage. Reports said that 60 British made it back from what is now called the Battle of Bloody Run.

This engraving shows Pontiac facing Major Gladwyn, as the British realize the Native Americans are not there for a friendly visit after all.

At Fort Michilimackinac in Michigan on June 2, 1763, the Ojibwe and Sauk tribes tricked soldiers there by playing a game of lacrosse. (The sport was first created by Native Americans and is still popular today.) Painting their bodies with clay and chalk, the warriors put on a show of athletics. The 30-year-old British Major George Etherington was perhaps naïve to believe that this was a mere sporting event. He opened the fort gates and allowed his 35 men to watch the spectacle. While they were preoccupied with the play, Indian women, draped in bulky blankets snuck into the fort. Etherington and his men were too engaged to question why they were wearing heavy blankets on a hot June day. Under their covers, the squaws had hidden knives and tomahawks. Once they were inside the gate, an Indian lacrosse player sent the leather lacrosse ball flying "mistakenly" into the fort. When players rushed for the ball, the women opened up their blankets and quickly distributed the weapons. Catching the British totally off guard, the Indians slaughtered most of the soldiers but spared French traders who were at the post.

Bloody skirmishes continued on both sides for the next three years. In the fall of 1764, Colonel Henry Bouquet, who had fought alongside Forbes at Fort Duquesne, led 1,500 men into Ohio to contain the Indians. He thought that Amherst's cold policies were to blame for the situation: "We have visibly brought upon us this Indian war by being too saving of a few presents to the savages, which properly distributed would certainly have prevented it."[4]

In the end, the British had more manpower and firepower than the Indians. On July 25, 1766, Potomac signed a peace treaty with the British. The treaty gave some minimal formal recognition to Indian land rights.

The End of the War

By the fall of 1762, Spain and France realized that their cause was hopeless. At the end of November, the final draft of the Treaty of Paris was presented. Great Britain would take all of Canada and France would give up all claims east of the Mississippi with the exception of New Orleans. France kept two small islands just south of Fortune, Newfoundland, in the northeast

Atlantic—Saint Pierre and Miquelon. (To this day, these tiny islands remain part of France as a self-governing *collectivité territoriale*. They only accept the European euro as currency.)[5] The British also allowed the French fishing rights in the Great Banks of Newfoundland. In the Caribbean, France would keep Guadeloupe, Martinique, and St. Lucia, while the British would take other islands in the area. Britain also strengthened holds in Africa and took control of much of India.

Spain gave up Florida to Britain, and in exchange kept Cuba and Manila. France agreed that all lands west of New Orleans, called Louisiana, should go to Spain. Britain and the colonies did not see much worth to this land at the time. In 1800, Napoleon of France would get Spain to give back Louisiana, which he would later to sell to the United States for the equivalent of about $15 million (including cancellation of French debts).

When the British took over, most Spanish in Florida left. However, most French settlers remained in Canada, Illinois, and Louisiana.

On February 10, 1763, Britain, France and Spain signed the Treaty of Paris at Versailles in France.[6] At the moment Britain stood proud and victorious having truly created a vast British Empire. Still, all was not stable for almighty England. As mentioned, fighting with the Indians continued, and the French and Indian War had

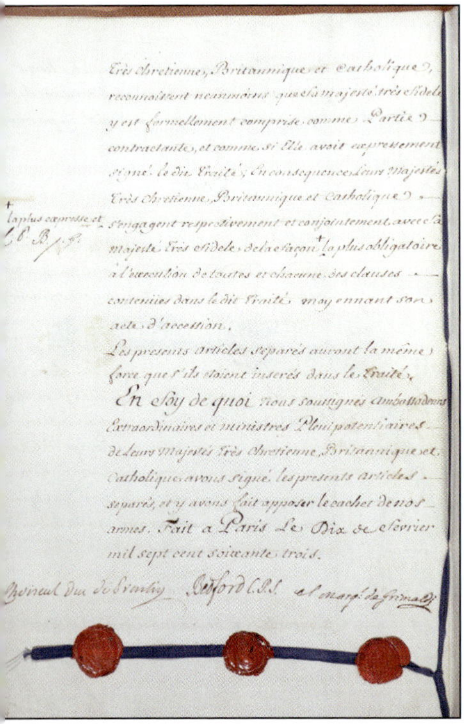

The Treaty of Paris was signed by France, Britain, and Spain, on February 10, 1763, to officially end the Seven Years' War.

sewn the seeds for the American Revolution. While the colonists and the British had to work together to stop the encroaching French, the battle brought to light potential friction.

How This War Led to a Revolution

Wanting to keep the peace with the Indians, King George III issued the Royal Proclamation of 1763 in October of that year. The decree forbade settlement past a line running along the Appalachian Mountains. It excluded the Ohio Valley. The colonists were just celebrating the opening of the frontier after winning the war, and now the king was limiting expansion. Many colonists felt Britain was trying to pen them in for better control. Resentment among the colonists grew.

After signing the treaty, more British soldiers arrived. Throughout the fighting, the British had a superior attitude over the colonists, and they lodged themselves in the homes of the settlers. In addition, Britain now was in desperate need of cash. Building an empire and a strong navy required a boatload of money, which put Britain into massive debt. England expected America to shoulder much of the expense. On April 5, 1764, Parliament passed the Sugar Act, formally known as the American Duties Act of 1764. Sugar, coffee, wine, and many other imports into the colonies would now be taxed, and collection of these taxes was strictly enforced. The legislation showed that Britain was increasing its involvement in colonial life, and it led to the protest cry, "no taxation without representation." Britain was taxing the colonies but they had no say in British policy. Then England passed the Stamp Act of 1765, imposing a tax on all paper—newspapers, legal documents, playing cards, etc. The Americans boycotted the act, and it was eventually repealed. But now the tensions between the colonies were escalating, and by 1775, Britain was at war with its American colonies.

On April 18, 1775, British soldiers set off from Boston to Concord, Massachusetts, to confiscate weapons and ammunitions stockpiled by the American colonists. At Lexington, they confronted local militiamen and a gun was fired. It was called the "shot heard around the world" and marked the beginning of the American Revolution.

Because of their defeat in the French and Indian War, France was eager to help the colonists when the American Revolution started.

They were happy to lend a hand against their rival, Britain. France provided the colonists with military armaments and loans. The country sent an estimated 12,000 soldiers and 32,000 sailors to the American war effort. Ben Franklin was instrumental in securing French support—on February 6, 1778, they signed the Treaty of Amity and Commerce and the Treaty of Alliance, making their collaborative efforts official.

The French who had remained in Canada, however, did not want to join the war effort because of concessions that the British made toward them. On June 22, 1774, parliament had passed the Quebec Act. It extended boundaries of the region west to the Mississippi, north to Hudson Bay and east to the St. Lawrence. The law also guaranteed religious freedom to the Catholic Canadians, although Quebec could not elect a legislative assembly—it was to be governed by an appointed governor and council.

Although the united colonies could not get the French Canadians to join their side, the support of France was critical to the birth of the United States, and it was their naval power that made a difference at a low point for the struggling colonies. With French assistance, Americans won a battle that many view as one of the most important of the Revolution.

In 1781, America and Britain had been at war for six years, and the Americans were suffering great losses. The British occupied New York City. In the south, they had captured Richmond and

The shots fired at Lexington and Concord would launch the colonists into the American Revolution, where they won their independence from Britain.

Charleston. With the aid of the French navy and additional French soldiers, General George Washington coordinated a devastating attack against Cornwallis and his 9,000 troops in Yorktown, Virginia, on September 28. Cornwallis surrendered. With this Patriot victory, it became clear to Britain that they could not defeat the colonists. This victory, due largely to French involvement, paved the way for peace negotiations, resulting in the liberty of the thirteen colonies, and the eventual birth of the United States of America. Today, in North America, we continue to see the legacy of the war with the vibrant French-influenced culture in New Orleans and Louisiana, as well as in Quebec City and Montreal to the north in Canada.

Chronology

1607—The British establish their first colony in North America—Jamestown in Virginia.

1608—The French establish their first colony in North America—Quebec in Canada.

1752–1753—The French build forts from New Orleans to Montreal.

December 1753—George Washington delivers a letter to the French at Fort Le Boeuf from Governor Robert Dinwiddie asking them to leave the Ohio Valley.

April 1754—The French start building Fort Duquesne at a critical fork of the Monongahela and Allegheny Rivers.

May 9, 1754—Ben Franklin publishes America's first political cartoon urging the colonies to "Join, or die!" as the French expanded their territory.

May 28, 1754—George Washington's firefight with French near Fort Duquesne begins the unofficial French and Indian War.

July 3, 1754—French defeat George Washington at Fort Necessity.

June–July 1754—Seven of the thirteen colonies unite at the Conference of Albany to try to stop the French and improve relations with Indians.

February 23, 1755—General Edward Braddock arrives in America to lead the British forces in the colonies.

June–July 1755—The British defeat the French in Nova Scotia and deport thousands of Acadians (French settlers). Many wind up moving to Louisiana and New Orleans.

July 9, 1755—General Braddock and British troops suffer a major loss while attempting to take Fort Duquesne. General Braddock dies from a bullet wound.

September 1755—The British win the Battle of Lake George.

November 13, 1755—Fort William Henry is completed.

May 15, 1756—Britain officially declares war on France.

August 15, 1756—The French capture Fort Oswego and burn it to the ground.

June 1757—William Pitt and the Duke of Newcastle form a new ministry in Britain. Pitt, as secretary of state, proves to be a decisive leader.

August 1757—Lord Loudoun, commander of British forces in North America, gives up plans to take Fort Louisbourg.

August 9, 1757—French leader Montcalm captures Fort William Henry on Lake George. The next day, Indians massacre British who have surrendered.

July 8, 1758—A small army of French led by Montcalm at Fort Carillon repel a major attack by the British.

July 26, 1758—Fort Louisbourg falls to the British.

August 25, 1758—The British easily overpower Frontenac on the St. Lawrence and burn it to the ground.

November 1758—The Cherokee and English fight against each other over land in the south.

November 24, 1758—Outnumbered by approaching British forces, the French burn Fort Duquesne and flee.

January 1, 1759—George Washington resigns from military service.

July 25, 1759—The British take Fort Niagara.

July 26, 1759—French blow up their own Fort Carillon as overwhelming numbers of British troops approach.

September 13, 1759—A decisive battle on the Plains of Abraham leads to the fall of Quebec. Both French commander Montcalm and British leader Major General James Wolfe die from battle wounds.

April 28, 1760—The French give a final push to recapture Quebec in the Battle of Sainte-Foy.

September 8, 1760—Vaudreuil, Governor of New France, surrenders the final stronghold, Montreal, and major fighting between the French and British ends.

August 15, 1761—Spain agrees to help France in war effort if needed.

November 1761—The Cherokee sign a peace treaty with British.

January 4, 1762—Britain declares war on Spain.

February 10, 1763—Britain, France, and Spain sign Treaty of Paris officially ending the war, giving huge territorial gains to Britain.

October 7, 1763—King George III issues the Proclamation of 1763 restricting settlement on the frontier west of the Appalachians.

May 7, 1763—Pontiac's Rebellion, involving tribes from many nations, begins. Coordinated attacks are launched on British forts.

June 2, 1763—Indian warriors use lacrosse game as a trick to enter Fort Michilimackinac in Michigan and kill soldiers there.

July 25, 1766—Potomac signs a peace treaty with British.

April 18, 1775—The American Revolution begins.

Chapter Notes

CHAPTER 1 COMING TO AMERICA

1. "Europe and the New World," *Le Canada: A People's History, CBC Learning,* retrieved January 18, 2016, http://www.cbc.ca/history/EPCONTENTSE1EP2CH1PA1LE.html.
2. *Explorers of America,* retrieved January 18, 2016, http://www.landofthebrave.info/american-history-of-early-explorers.htm.
3. Dirk J. Barreveld, *Henry Hudson and the Rise and Fall of New Amsterdam, Lulu.com,* 2009, p. 221, http://www.lulu.com/shop/dr-dirk-j-barreveld/henry-hudson-and-the-rise-and-fall-of-new-amsterdam/ebook/product-20852520.html.
4. Harold Horwood, *Plunder and Pillage: Atlantic Canada's Brutal and Bloodthirsty Pirates and Privateers* (Nova Scotia, Canada: Formac Publishing, 2011), p. 60.
5. Charles C. Mann, "1492," *The Atlantic,* March 2002, retrieved January 18, 2016, http://www.theatlantic.com/magazine/archive/2002/03/1491/302445/.
6. Paul Boyer, Clifford Clark, Joseph Kett, Neal Salisbury, and Harvard Sitkoff, *The Enduring Vision: A History of the American People* (New York: Houghton Mifflin, 2008), p. 96.
7. Bishop David Arias, *The Martyrs of the United States* (Morrisville, NC: Lulu Press, 2012), p. 106.
8. Elizabeth MacLeod and Frieda Wishinsky, *A History of Just About Everything* (Toronto, Canada: Kids Can Press, 2013), p. 49.
9. Francis Drake and F.J. Dowd, *Indian History for Young Folks* (New York: Harper & Brothers, 1885), pp. 181–185.
10. "War of the Spanish Succession," *Encyclopedia Britannica,* updated July 24, 2014, retrieved January 18, 2016, http://www.britannica.com/event/War-of-the-Spanish-Succession.

CHAPTER 2 THE SETTLEMENTS GROW

1. Paul Boyer, Clifford Clark, Joseph Kett, Neal Salisbury, and Harvard Sitkoff, *The Enduring Vision: A History of the American People* (New York: Houghton Mifflin, 2008), p. 71.
2. Julie Anne Sweet, "War of Jenkins' Ear," *New Georgia Encyclopedia.* Written February 13, 2003. Edited September 9, 2015. Retrieved July 18, 2016, http://www.georgiaencyclopedia.org/articles/history-archaeology/war-jenkins-ear.
3. "War of the Austrian Succession," *Encyclopedia Britannica.* Last updated July 24, 2014 Retrieved July 18, 2016, http://www.britannica.com/event/War-of-the-Austrian-Succession.
4. Luther C. Leavitt, "The Siege of Louisbourg," *The Order of the Founders and Patriots of America,* retrieved January 18, 2016, http://www.founderspatriots.org/articles/louisbourg.php.
5. Alan Axelrod, *American Revolution: A New Look at the Past* (New York: Sterling Publishing, 2007), p. 34.
6. "Celeron de Bienville," *Ohio History Connection,* retrieved January 18, 2016, http://www.ohiohistorycentral.org/w/Celeron_de_Bienville.
7. Philip S. Klein and Ari Hoogenboom, *A History of Pennsylvania* (University Park, Pennsylvania: The Pennsylvania State University Press, 1973).

CHAPTER 3 GEORGE WASHINGTON IGNITES A WAR

1. Robert M. McClung, *Young George Washington and the French and Indian War 1753-1758* (North Haven, Connecticut: Linnet Book, 2002), pp. 1–12.
2. Allan Gallay, *Colonial Wars of North America* (New York: Routledge, 2015).
3. McClung, p. 50.

4. Kennedy Hickman, "French and Indian War: Fort Necessity and the Battle of Great Meadows," *About Education.* Updated May 6, 2015. Retrieved January 18, 2016, http://militaryhistory.about.com/od/battleswars16011800/p/fortnecessity.htm.

CHAPTER 4 A STORM ON THE HORIZON

1. Walter R. Borneman, *The French & Indian War: Deciding the Fate of North America* (New York: Harper Collins, 2006), pp. 25-40.
2. Richard Cavendish, "General Braddock Defeated," *History Today,* July 7, 2005, retrieved January 18, 2016, http://www.historytoday.com/richard-cavendish/general-braddock-defeated.
3. Shane K. Bernard, *Cajuns and Their Acadian Ancestors: A Young Reader's History* (Jackson, Mississippi: University Press of Mississippi/Jackson, 2008), pp. 70–72.
4. William Wilson, "Braddock's Debacle," *Historical Narratives of Early Canada,* retrieved January 18, 2016, http://www.uppercanadahistory.ca/uel/uelbrad.
5. William Fowler, *Empires at War* (New York: Walker & Company, 2005), p. 111.
6. "The Seven Years' War Begins," *History.com,* retrieved January 18, 2016, http://www.history.com/this-day-in-history/the-seven-years-war-begins.

CHAPTER 5 THE SHIFTING BALANCE OF POWER

1. R. Douglas Francis, Richard Jones, and Donald Smith, *Journeys: History of Canada* (Scarborough, Ontario: Nelson Education, 2010), pp. 88–89.
2. "Francois Bigot," *Dictionary of Canadian Biography,* University of Toronto, 1979. Retrieved January 18, 2016, http://www.biographi.ca/en/bio/bigot_francois_1778_4E.html.
3. Daniel Baugh, *The Global Seven Years' War, 1754–1763* (New York, Routledge, 2014), p. 198.
4. "The Loss of New France," *Heritage History,* retrieved January 18, 2016, http://www.heritage-history.com/?c=read&author=home&book=canada&story=loss.

5. "The History," *Relive: Bring History to Life,* retrieved January 18, 2016, http://www.warforempire.org/relive/the_history.aspx.
6. "Fort William Henry Massacre," United States History, retrieved January 18, 2016, http://www.u-s-history.com/pages/h1175.html.

CHAPTER 6 THE BRITISH STAR RISES

1. "The History," *Relive: Bring History to Life,* retrieved January 18, 2016, http://www.warforempire.org/relive/the_history.aspx.
2. William R. Nester, *The First Global War: Britain, France, and the Fate of North America, 1756–1775* (Westport, Connecticut: Praeger Publishers, 2000), p. 92.
3. "Deportation and New Settlement 1755–1810," *Grand Pré,* retrieved January 18, 2016, http://www.landscapeofgrandpre.ca/deportation-and-new-settlement-1755ndash1810.html.
4. "Fort Carillon," *United States History,* retrieved January 18, 2016, http://www.u-s-history.com/pages/h1174.html.
5. "John Bradstreet," *Ohio History Connection,* retrieved January 18, 2016, http://www.ohiohistorycentral.org/w/John_Bradstreet.
6. "Fort Ligonier," *Fort Ligonier,* retrieved January 18, 2016, http://fortligonier.org/history/fort-ligonier/.
7. "Forbes Trail," *Relive,* retrieved January 18, 2016, http://www.warforempire.org/visit/forbes_trail.aspx.

CHAPTER 7 THE FALL OF NEW FRANCE

1. "History of Old Fort Niagara," *Old Fort Niagara,* retrieved January 18, 2016, http://www.oldfortniagara.org/history.
2. "Fort Carillon," *United States History,* retrieved January 18, 2016, http://www.u-s-history.com/pages/h1174.html.
3. William Wood, *The Winning of Canada: A Chronicle of Wolfe* (Toronto: Glasgow, Brook & Company, 1922), pp. 70–71.

4. "Battle of the Plains of Abraham," *Historica Canada,* retrieved January 18, 2016, http://www.thecanadianencyclopedia.ca/en/article/battle-of-the-plains-of-abraham/.
5. Wood, p. 129.
6. "Reinforcements From Europe: Battle of Ste. Foy," *Le Canada,* retrieved January 18, 2016, http://www.cbc.ca/history/EPCONTENTSE1EP4CH10PA2LE.html.
7. "French Surrender at Montreal," *Le Canada,* retrieved January 18, 2016, http://www.cbc.ca/history/EPCONTENTSE1EP4CH10PA3LE.html.
8. "French and Indian War/Seven Years' War, 1754–63," *U.S. Department of State: Office of the Historian,* retrieved January 18, 2016, https://history.state.gov/milestones/1750-1775/french-indian-war.

CHAPTER 8 THE FINAL STAGES

1. "Attakullakulla 'Little Carpenter' Onacona, Ukwaniequa Moytoy (Uku of Tanasi), Cherokee Emissary to England," *Geni,* retrieved January 19, 2016, http://www.geni.com/people/Attakullakulla-Onacona/n6000000011727533816.
2. Joe Guy, *The Hidden History of Southeast Tennessee* (Charleston, South Carolina: The History Press, 2011), pp. 34–37.
3. "Conspiracy of Pontiac," *History of the USA,* retrieved January 19, 2016, http://www.usahistory.info/French-Indian-War/Pontiac.html.
4. Lissa Edwards, "Deadly Lacrosse Game in Mackinac Straits at Fort Michilimackinac in 1763," *MyNorth,* May 16, 2010, retrieved January 19, 2016, http://mynorth.com/2010/05/deadly-lacrosse-game-in-mackinac-straits-at-fort-michilimackinac-in-1763/.
5. "St. Pierre and Miquelon," retrieved January 19, 2016, http://st-pierre-et-miquelon.com/en/.
6. "The French and Indian War Ends," *History.com,* retrieved January 19, 2016, http://www.history.com/this-day-in-history/the-french-and-indian-war-ends.

Glossary

allegiance—Loyalty or commitment to a nation, sovereign, individual, or cause

artillery—Large-caliber weapons, such as cannon, howitzers, and missile launchers, that are operated by crews

bateaux—A light flat-bottomed riverboat used in eastern and central North America

capitulation—An agreement in time of war to terms of surrender to a hostile armed force

confederation—An organization that consists of a number of parties or groups united to form an alliance

consumption—A wasting disease, especially pulmonary tuberculosis

formidable—Causing fear or respect through being impressively large, powerful, intense, or capable.

frigate—A medium-sized square-rigged warship of the 18th and 19th centuries

longhouse—The traditional dwelling of the Iroquois and other North American Indians

militiamen—A body of citizens enrolled for military service, as opposed to regular who are professional, full-time military personnel

missionary—A person sent on a religious mission, especially one sent to promote Christianity in a foreign country

regiment—A unit of ground forces, usually consisting of two or more battalions or battle groups, a headquarters unit, and specific supporting units

regulars—Professional soldiers in a permanently organized *army* of a country

succession—A typical order through which the crown is passed down from one royal family member to another

For More Information

Books

Horn, Bernd. *Battle Cries in the Wilderness: The Struggle for North America in the Seven Years' War.* Toronto: Dundurn, 2011.

Middlekauf, Robert. *Washington's Revolution: The Making of America's First Leader*. New York: Vintage/Random House, 2016

Preston, David. *Braddock's Defeat: The Battle of the Monongahela and the Road to Revolution*. Oxford, UK: Oxford University Press, 2015.

Websites

The French and Indian War in Pennsylvania, ExplorePAHistory.com
explorepahistory.com/story.php?storyId=1-9-6
Gives in-depth information about the French and Indian War in Pennsylvania.

French and Indian War/Seven Years' War, 1754–63, US Department of State
history.state.gov/milestones/1750-1775/french-indian-war
Provides information about the war.

Movies

The War That Made America. PBS, 2006.
www.wqed.org/tv/specials/the-war-that-made-america/index_12.php
A dramatic documentary on the French and Indian War.

Last of the Mohicans. 1992
The film tells the story of three trappers during the French and Indian War.

Index

A

Abercromby, James, 77–78, 80–81, 90, 92
Acadians, 10, 21, 50, 52–54, 116, 121
Algonquin Indians, 13, 15, 38
American Duties Act, 113
American Revolution, 5, 49, 60, 87, 112–113, 115, 118, 120
Amherst, Jeffrey 76, 78, 90–93, 106–107, 110
Attakullakulla, 103, 104, 106, 123

B

battle of
  Bloody Marsh, 26
  Bloody Run, 109
  Carillon, 78
  Lake George, 58–59, 117
Beaujeu, Daniel Liénard de, 55, 56
Bigot, Francois, 64, 121
Bouquet, Henry, 82–84, 110
Braddock, Edward, 50–52, 54–58, 69, 82, 84, 116
Braddock's Road, 54, 83
Britain, 7, 27, 29, 35, 49, 60–61, 69, 94, 99–100, 110–15, 117–118, 122

C

Cabot, John, 8–9
Canada, 4, 9, 12, 17, 20, 22, 60, 65–66, 73, 90, 92–94, 99, 110–11, 114–116, 118–19, 121–122
cartoon, first American political, 41, 42
Cayugas Indians, 13, 16
Cherokee Indians, 13, 103–106, 117–118
Clark, Clifford, 119
Colonies, 18, 28, 41, 47–52, 66, 69, 73, 84, 89, 91, 111, 113–116
  American, 29, 113
  British, 9, 24, 65, 94
  British American, 29
  Dutch, 10
  English, 20, 24–25, 29, 47
  French, 9
  Spanish, 24
  Thirteen, 12, 47
Conference of Albany, 47, 49, 116
Contrecoeur, Captain Pierre de, 40, 55

D

Deadly Lacrosse Game, 109–110
Dinwiddie, Robert, 30, 35, 38–40, 43, 45, 59
Drucour, Augustin de Boschenry de, 75–76
Duquesne, Michel–Ange, 33, 38

E

Easton Treaty, 85, 91
England, 5, 7–10, 12, 17–21, 23–25, 27, 28, 30, 33, 47, 50, 52, 60, 66, 67, 69, 72, 85, 89, 93, 97, 99, 101, 103, 111, 113
Etherington, George, 109
Europe, 8, 17, 19–20, 26, 30, 68, 72, 122

F

Family Compact, 100
Forbes, John, 82–83, 85–86, 91, 104, 110
Forbes Road, 83, 91
forts 4, 6, 14, 25, 30, 32–35, 37–40, 49, 66, 76, 81–83, 85, 87, 91–92, 108–110, 116–117
  Beauséjour, 51–52
  Carillon, 70, 75, 77–78, 80, 82, 90, 92, 117, 122
  Cumberland, 54, 59
  Detroit, 99, 108

Duquesne, 40–44, 50–52, 54–56, 60, 75, 82–87, 104, 110, 116–117
Edward, 58, 70–71
Frontenac, 65, 81, 89
Le Boeuf, 33–35, 37, 39, 116
Ligonier, 83–84
Louisbourg, 21, 28, 50, 69, 74–76, 93, 117
Michilimackinac, 109, 118
Necessity, 41, 43–45, 50–51, 55, 60, 116
Niagara, 25, 50–51, 57, 81, 89–92, 108, 117, 122
Ontario, 65–66
Oswego, 57, 65–66, 117
Pitt, 87, 108
Presque Isle, 33, 108
Prince George, 104–106
Saint-Frédéric 25, 50, 51, 57–58, 70, 90, 93
William Henry, 58, 70–71, 76, 78, 81, 117
France, 5, 7, 9–10, 12, 14, 17, 19, 21, 24–27, 29–30, 60–61, 65–68, 99–101, 110–114, 117–118
Franklin, Benjamin 33, 46, 114, 116, 41–42, 49
French and Indian War, 4–5, 7, 14, 24, 26, 29, 41, 46, 60–62, 67–68, 77, 96, 100, 111, 113, 116

G

Galissonnière, 22, 30–32
Gist, Christopher, 32, 35, 39
Gladwyn, Henry 108–109
Great Expulsion, 52

H

Half-King, 34, 36–37, 39, 42–43
Haudenosaunee, 16. See also Six Nations; Iroquois Confederacy.
Howe, William, 78, 79
Huron Indians, 16, 108

I

Indians, 5–6, 12–14, 18, 31–33, 36–37, 42–45, 48–49, 54–55, 59, 65–66, 70–72, 84–87, 91–92, 104–8, 110–112
Iroquois Confederacy, 16, 34, 48–49
Iroquois Indians, 13, 16–17, 29, 33, 36, 44, 49, 84, 91–92, 124

J

Jonquière, 32–33
Jumonville, Coulon de Villiers, Sieur de, 42–43, 45

K

King George III, 106, 112, 118
King George's War, 26–29, 47
King Louis XV, 99, 100
King Philip's War, 47
King William III, 18
King William's War, 17

L

L'Anse au Foulon, 95
Lawrence, Charles, 36, 52
Lévis, Francois de, 98–99
Lignery, Francois-Marie le Marchand de, 83, 86
Loudoun, Lord, 59, 69–70, 117
Lyttelton, William, 105, 106

M

Marchand, Francois-Marie le, 83
Marin, Pierre-Paul, 3
Mi'kmaq Indians, 27, 28, 50
Minorca, 61, 66, 100
Mississaugas Indians, 55
Mississippi, 12, 25, 29, 104, 110, 114, 121
Montcalm, Louis-Joseph, 61, 63–66, 68, 70–72, 77–79, 81–82, 89–90, 93, 96–97, 117
Montreal, 4, 9, 33, 81, 97–100, 106, 115–116, 118
Murray, James, 98–99

N

Native Americans, 5, 12, 14–16, 20, 30, 32, 101, 109
New France, 12–13, 18, 21–22, 24–26, 30, 32–33, 38, 40, 61, 63–64, 67–68, 73, 81–82, 89–90, 106
New Orleans, 12, 23, 33, 110–11, 115–116
New York, 4, 10, 16, 18, 25, 47, 48, 51, 59, 70, 78, 90, 93, 108, 114
Nine Years' War, 17–18
North America, 5, 7–10, 12, 24–25, 29, 66–69, 73, 77, 90, 93–94, 115, 117, 120, 122, 125
Nova Scotia, 8, 10, 18, 20–21, 27–28, 50, 52, 69, 77, 119

O

Oglethorpe, James, 25–26,
Ohio Indians, 84–85
Onondaga Indians, 13, 16
Ottawa Indians, 55, 102, 108

P

Pelham–Holles, Thomas, 67
Pepperrell, William, 28
Phips, William, 18
Pierre, Jacques Legardeur de Saint, 38
Pitt, William, 62, 67–68, 72–73, 75, 90, 93, 100, 117
Plains of Abraham, 95–96, 98, 117
Pontiac, 107–109
Potawatomi Indians, 55, 108
Pottawatomie Indians, 102
Prideaux, John, 91, 92

Q

Quebec, 4, 9, 18, 21, 32, 50, 68, 76, 88, 93–99, 114, 116–118
Quebec Act, 114
Queen Anne's War, 20, 47

S

Seven Years' War, 61, 100, 112
Shirley, William, 27
Sioux Indians, 13
Spain, 8, 12–13, 17, 19, 21, 25, 29, 60, 100–101, 110–112, 118
Stamp Act, 42, 113
Stobo, Robert, 45, 52

T

Tanacharison, 34, 37, 39, 41–43
Toronto, 32, 119, 121–22, 125
treaty, 21, 37, 85, 106, 110–112
  of Aix–la–Chappelle, 28
  of Alliance, 114
  of Amity and Commerce, 114
  of Easton, 91
  of Lancaster, 29
  of Paris, 110
  of Ryswick, 19
  of Toronto,
  of Utrecht, 2

V

Van Braam, 36, 44
Vandreuil, 89–90
Virginia, 9, 29–30, 35–36, 40, 50, 69, 108, 115–116
Virginia assembly, 69

W

Waldron, Richard, 17, 18
War of the Austrian Succession, 26, 60, 64
War of Jenkin's Ear, 25–26, 29
War of the League of Augsburg, 17
War of Spanish Succession, 20
Washington, George, 3, 36–37, 39–45, 50–51, 55–57, 59–60, 65, 82–83, 85–87, 115–117
Wolfe, General James, 65, 75, 88, 93–98, 117
Wyandot Indians, 55